ART
CAREER
GUIDE

ART CAREER GUIDE

Second Edition:
Revised and Enlarged
A Guidance Handbook
for Art Students, Teachers,
Vocational Counselors,
and Job Hunters

by Donald Holden

Watson-Guptill Publications

For Willi

706.9
H69a

64277

December, 1968

© 1961 by Watson-Guptill Publications
New York, New York
Edited by Sterling McIlhany
Designed by James Craig
All rights reserved. Printed in U.S.A.
Library of Congress Catalog Card Number 61-18280
First edition, 1961
Printings 1961, 1963, 1965
Second edition, 1967

Acknowledgments

Many distinguished men and women in the fields of art, education, and publishing played vital roles in the publication of *Art Career Guide*. They generously served as advisers, critics, and sources of material. The author is grateful for the time and patience of James M. Alexander, Jr., Richard F. Bach, Ralph G. Beelke, Regina Benedict, Phillip A. Bruno, Arnold Buchheimer, Margaret Burlin, John Canaday, Howard Conant, Charles M. Dorn, Arthur S. Douglass, Jr., Henry Dreyfuss, John Ebstein, Cyril Lee Ellison, Yvonne Freund, Guy Fry, William Goldsmith, Richard Grossman, Dione Guffey, Robert B. Hale, William D. Hamilton, Robert Kaupelis, Norman Kent, Jean Koefoed, Boris Kroll, Ramah Larisch, Jack Lenor Larsen, Leo Lionni, Tran Mawicke, Sterling McIlhany, Sol Mednick, Joyce Morrow, Elias Newman, Jules Perel, Barye Phillips, Paul Reilly, Ben Rose, Norman Ulrich, and Polly Weaver.

Special thanks are due to my wife, Willi, who compiled the school lists, the most exasperating and most important job of all.

Cooperating organizations

The publication of *Art Career Guide* was made possible, in part, by the aid of leading professional organizations and government agencies. Many of these provided invaluable research material. Others gave advice and encouragement. Still others checked chapters for accuracy and completeness. The author is grateful for the cooperation of the following organizations:

American Association of University Professors
American Institute of Architects, New York Chapter
American Institute of Graphic Arts
American Institute of Interior Designers
American Personnel and Guidance Association
American Society of Magazine Photographers
Artists Equity Association, New York Chapter
Bureau of Labor Statistics, United States Department of Labor
Council of Industrial Design, London
Industrial Designers' Society of America
National Architectural Accrediting Board
National Art Education Association
National Education Association
National Society of Art Directors
National Society of Interior Designers
Office of Education, United States Department of Health, Education and Welfare
Professional Photographers of America
Society of Illustrators

Preface to second edition

Books go out of date not only because times change and facts change, but because the *author* changes.

Since *Art Career Guide* first appeared in 1961, the art professions have changed and so have the art schools. To bring this book up to date, the original text has been reread by the professional associations that cooperated so generously in the research for the first edition. Their suggested changes and additions have been incorporated in the new, revised edition of *Art Career Guide*.

One of the most popular features of the first edition was the art school directory. On the basis of a questionnaire survey of every art school, college, and university in America, this section has been updated and enlarged.

I began by saying that *authors* change. Rereading the original text, I must admit that some of my assertions now seem debatable. Over the years, I've changed my mind about some things—for the better, I hope. Thus, if you own the *first* edition of *Art Career Guide* and you've now replaced it with the *revised* edition, don't be surprised to find new opinions—as well as new facts—in the pages you're about to read.

Contents

Part One
Planning Your Education

1
How to use this book

One Sunday evening toward the end of high school, I interrupted dinner with a startling announcement: I wanted to become an artist.

This was an uneasy moment for my parents. Like most people, they had never really known any artists. The only artists they had ever seen were in the movies. And the Hollywood version of the artist was no one to envy. He was skinny, unshaven, hungry. True, the script gave him his quota of beautiful models. But this didn't seem to make him any happier. His eyes were daubed with shadowy makeup to give him that haunted, doomed look. His masterpieces lay scattered about his dingy studio, unsold. If fame and fortune did reach him at last, they came too late. The prices of his pictures always soared the day after his funeral. Was this what I expected to do with my life? My parents shook their heads.

No, I was sure the movies were wrong. I just couldn't believe that all artists were penniless Bohemians who died before their time. Certainly there was *some* way for a young artist to earn a living. There *had* to be.

My family had no contact with the art world, but even they knew the names of a few artists who were said to command thousands of dollars for a single canvas, just to hang in someone's living room. What about the illustrations we saw in magazines and newspapers? Weren't artists paid to draw them? What about our furniture, our drapes, our wallpaper? Didn't somebody have to design them? Come to think of it, someone had to design our apartment house too. Even an architect was an artist, though it had never occurred to us before.

My parents were encouraged. There was hope after all. It began to dawn on us, as we spoke, that there were many kinds of artists and all sorts of art careers. But how do you find out what these careers are? And how do you pick the right one? What do you study and how do you pick the right school? Then how do you find a job?

We hadn't the vaguest idea how to answer these questions. The next day, I went to the local library to look for a book that might help. There were plenty of books about jobs and schools. But amazingly enough, among those thousands of pages of advice, there was almost nothing about art careers. The branch librarian, who had worked hard to build up her guidance shelf, confirmed this. She told me there were lots of how-to-do-it books: richly illustrated textbooks on the techniques of drawing, painting, and various crafts. A few had chapters on job hunting. But my first job hunt was years off. There was no book to help me *now*.

Later that week, I tried the guidance counselor of my high school. He was a dedicated, overworked man, doing his best to keep up with all the printed matter that came across his desk. His walls were lined with books and college catalogs. He lent me catalogs he had collected from nearby art schools. He had made a point of visiting these schools periodically and talking to the instructors. He told me what he knew about art careers and art schools, but he frankly admitted that he couldn't tell me enough. He was well informed about professions like medicine and engineering. He had plenty of reading matter about these fields. Besides, he had friends in these professions. But his personal contact with artists was too infrequent. And like the librarian, he had no book to help him advise me.

My high school art teacher was eager to help. He was a good painter and knew his way around the art galleries. His illustrations had appeared in books and magazines, so he knew the publishing business. He told me all he could about these fields. But he added that there were many other art jobs he knew almost nothing about. He mentioned art careers I had never even heard of, like industrial design. But he was quick to admit that he was short on details.

And so I went on button-holing anyone who might have a few facts. I talked the ears off exasperated neighbors who happened to be Sunday painters. I went to the local art schools and gave patient teachers the third degree. And I hungrily combed art school catalogs and art textbooks for a few sentences of advice.

It was a slow, painful, haphazard search. Looking back on those discouraging days, I'm amazed that I didn't just give up. Somehow, I stumbled into the right school and the right profession. And by some miracle, I got a job, after a long, badly managed job hunt.

My days of painful groping were typical of art students then and *now*. Each year, I meet scores of art students and young job hunters who seem as ill-informed as I was. Our vocational guidance methods have improved enormously. There are whole libraries of "career books." But somehow the art profession has been left out. Maybe we have a romantic feeling that artists aren't guided by facts, but by the stars. Whatever the reason, facts about art careers are still hard to find.

The purpose of this book is to assemble these facts in one small package. Not *all* the facts, of course. No one knows all the facts, and no single book could hold them. But this brief handbook contains the basic facts I wish I had when I began my own art career.

A word to the student

This book is meant to guide you from your high school days, through your years of professional training in art school, to the time when you go out to find your first job.

The next chapter will help you decide whether a career in art is really for you. The following two chapters will tell you how to plan your high school program, then how to pick the right art school, college or university art department.

Then there's a series of chapters, each describing one of the major art fields you may enter. The nine fields are: fine art, which includes painting, sculpture, and printmaking; illustration; graphic design, sometimes called advertising design; fabric design; interior design; architecture; industrial design; photography; and art teaching. Within these chapters, you'll find facts about specialized offshoots of each field. For example, the fine art chapter discusses such specialties as portrait and mural painting. The chapter on illustration touches on book and fashion illustration. The graphic design chapter mentions such diverse careers as package and book design. Without getting lost in detail, I've tried to define each field-within-a-field. The section closes with a chapter on artists' incomes.

The next four chapters will tell you how to organize your job hunt. One chapter gives detailed instructions to help you write a resume of your qualifications. A second chapter suggests ways of planning your job campaign. The third chapter contains pointers on preparing a portfolio of your work. And the final chapter in this section discusses how to conduct yourself when you arrive at the big moment: the job interview.

The book concludes with a directory of art schools, colleges, and universities that offer professional courses in the nine career fields. The schools are listed by state, to help you find the ones nearest your home.

Some advice to parents

This book was written to encourage you. These twenty brief chapters should reassure you that there's a place in the world for your youngster's talent *if* he has what it takes.

This book gives you a means of helping him find that place. I suggest you read along with him. Since you may carry the cost of his four or five years in art school, it's natural for you to feel involved in the decisions he makes about his career and his professional school.

These decisions demand a lot of self-knowledge, perhaps more self-knowledge than many students have. This book is meant to help the young reader get to know himself. In the process, he's going to do plenty of thinking out loud. He's going to ask himself, and you, a lot of difficult questions. Like him, you won't know all the answers. You'll find many of the answers in this book, though not *all* of them. Too many questions are uniquely personal. They're questions that the young reader must answer for himself, with the help of a good sounding board: you. This book should help you become a better sounding board, the most vital role you can play in the life of a young artist struggling to find himself.

The book should also help you perform other services. It may help you advise your teenager on his high school course schedule. If you visit art schools—and I think you *should* if you have the time—you'll be better prepared to ask the right questions there. You'll also be a more astute judge of the answers. The concluding chapters may even suggest ways of helping your young artist find a job.

You need no art training to read this book. The text contains very little shop talk. Whenever technical terms are used, for lack of simpler words, they're explained in the text.

Suggestions for teachers, guidance counselors, and librarians

This is both a reference book and an informal textbook. You can dip into it to find the answer to a specific question. Or you can read the text as a continuous "story."

A true reference book is organized in a way that makes facts easy to find when you want them. This volume tries to achieve this in two ways. First, the sequence of chapters and chapter subdivisions follows an obvious logic: the facts are where the reader expects to find them. Second, the format is designed to make facts accessible. Though the "story line" is continuous, there are a great many "heads" and "subheads" within each chapter.

On the other hand, I've said this is a textbook. I do hope these pages will make lively reading. Though it's more informal than most textbooks, I think you'll find the book useful as a classroom tool or for outside assignments. The contents and reading level are geared to the high school art major and the art school student. Probably the ideal time to assign the book would be the final year of high school or the freshman year of art school, when the student has to choose his major subject.

Individual chapters can be assigned when they relate to current class projects. Or the chapters can be read consecutively. I think it's best to read Part Two—the chapters that describe the major art fields—in quick succession. This helps the student to compare the various careers while they're all fresh in his mind.

As a counseling tool, this book is something you can assign to parents as well as students. In my experience, one of the common counseling problems is that the student, ill-informed as he may be, still knows more about art careers than his family does. The parents feel helpless. They don't feel equipped to advise their youngster because they just don't have enough facts. They're intimidated by all the half truths and pseudo-professional lingo their teenager has begun to build up. For these parents, the book can be a short course to strengthen their confidence and bridge the gap that divides them from the son or daughter they want to help.

Help for mature job hunters

Though this book stresses the vocational problems of young people, the mature job hunter will also find help here. This is the man who's unhappy in one line of work and wants to try another. He may be working in one art field and want to switch to a different art career. Or he may not be an artist at all. An art career may be a totally new idea in his life.

Switches like these are common. My own circle of friends includes an engineer who became an architect, then turned to industrial design; an industrial designer who changed to graphic design and is now art director of a national magazine; a successful art director who quit his job to teach and paint; a painter who became a leading advertising photographer. And I know dozens of others.

If you're thinking of making such a change, but you're not sure which art field is the right one, this book may help. The chapters in Part Two will help you compare various art jobs with your present job. As you read these chapters, you may discover that you need more schooling. If so, you'll want to examine the school directory section and the chapter on picking an art school.

For someone who's already in an art job, the chapters on job hunting *may* seem unnecessary. Having interviewed hundreds of job hunting artists, designers, and architects, I've been astonished to see how badly most job campaigns are managed. Seasoned professionals often act like disorganized amateurs when the time comes to plan a job campaign. The final chapters of this book explain how to *program* your hunt, to find the right job in the shortest time.

A word to the maverick

When he heard that this book was under way, one noted art director asked: "What about the maverick, the off-beat guy who doesn't fit anything you say, whom no book can help because he's unique?"

Among thousands of artists and art students, there's always the rare bird. There's always the man who has a unique contribution to make. We can make generalizations that fit most artists and art students, but these generalizations don't fit *him*. He defies classification. He's like no one else. And for just this reason, he often has a long struggle to find himself. He's like a sculptor I know, who spent years shaping statues, until one day he discovered that he really wanted to shape visionary wooden houses with his own hands. The maverick may waste years trying to be what he *isn't*, until at last he discovers what he *is*.

Is it really true that no book can help him? I think there *is* one basic service that this book may perform.

My daughter was once given a book about a little animal who awoke, one morning, from his long winter sleep and couldn't recall what kind of animal he was. He went through the forest asking other animals, "Can you tell me what I am?" None of them knew. Someone suggested he go to the zoo, which housed all the animals in the world. There he would surely find other animals like himself.

So he went to the zoo and patiently walked from cage to cage. He looked at lions, tigers, elephants, zebras, giraffes. But none of them looked like him. Finally, the wise owl looked at him carefully and said: "Why don't you go over and see the bears. You look to me like a kind of a bear." He went to the bears and they agreed. He was a kind of a bear. But what kind? He wasn't like the other bears. He was different. The oldest and wisest of the bears thought the problem over and solved it very simply. "You're not a kind of a bear," he said. "You're a Very Special Kind of a Bear." Our hero was satisfied. He returned to the forest and lived happily ever after, being just what he was: a Very Special Kind of a Bear.

The Very Special Kind of an Artist may find it worthwhile to tour this book as my daughter's bear toured the zoo. If the book does nothing else for you, it may tell you all the things you aren't. Knowing what you *aren't*, you may find it easier to decide what you *are*.

Future editions of this book

Like most books, this one probably contains its share of errors and omissions. Every word has been checked by experts: leading artists, educators, and professional organizations. But even this doesn't mean the book is without flaws. Every book can be improved and this one is no exception to the rule.

In future editions of *Art Career Guide*, I hope to make these improvements with your help. If you have suggestions to make about the next edition, though it may be a few years off, I hope you'll take the time to drop a note to the publisher. He'll forward your note to me.

2
Should you
become an artist?

How do you know you're cut out to be an artist? For some
readers, the answer is simple. They just *know*, that's all. They've
always wanted to be artists. They've never even considered any
other career. But for many readers, life isn't that simple.

There are so many things that may confuse the issue. What
if your high school report card says you're good at several
things? You get good grades in art, but you also get them in
English, history, languages. Maybe you should be a journalist,
teach history, enter the foreign service. Or your father's a
doctor; you've always admired him and you wonder if you'd
make a good doctor too. Perhaps you built your own hi-fi set
last summer; it was so much fun, you wonder if you might enjoy
being an engineer. And what if there's a profitable family business? Your family might be happy if you went to work for
Uncle Pete.

Despite all these distracting possibilities, how can you tell
you're really an artist at heart? Are there any special signs, any
characteristics that artists have, even in their teens?

It's fair to say that most artists, designers, and architects have
certain traits in common. In this chapter, I'll try to tell you
what some of these traits are. But as you read, remember there's
no law that says a successful artist *must* have all these qualities.
No two artists are alike. This chapter isn't a test you must pass.
I know several first rate artists, designers, and architects who
might not pass. But if you *do* have many of the qualities described here, you should feel encouraged.

Is there an artistic temperament?

One popular idea about artists is that they have something called artistic temperament. Artists are said to be moody, unpredictable, hot-tempered. There are just enough legends to keep this idea alive. Michelangelo is said to have thrown a paint pot at the Pope. Leonardo da Vinci got bored with many of his greatest paintings and never finished them. Cézanne, we're told, tossed his masterpieces into the bushes and his wife went out to retrieve them. And it seems to be true that Van Gogh sliced off an ear.

But despite these tales, some true, some false, artistic temperament is a poor test of talent. In fact, I doubt that artists are really more temperamental than other professional groups. The most erratic people *I've* met aren't artists at all. They're waiters. If you live in an apartment house, *your* candidate for the temperament prize is probably your building superintendent. And any businessman will tell you how many moody salesmen he's worked with.

In short, artists have no corner on temperament. It's just that nobody makes movies or writes magazine stories about hot-tempered cab drivers. The exploits of artists make more glamorous material.

There are other stereotypes about so-called artistic temperament that need puncturing. We're told that artists are impractical, that they're bad businessmen. We're told that they're bad organizers, bad administrators. Yet it's obvious that there are thousands of highly paid artists, designers, and architects who couldn't have succeeded if they weren't effective businessmen, meeting deadlines, collecting their bills, organizing their own efforts, and directing the work of others.

We're told that artists are irresponsible dreamers who neglect their families and would rather paint than eat. Yet most artists are as happily married as other people, hold down good jobs, feed and clothe their children, and manage to send them through college. I know hundreds of artists and few of them look underfed.

So then, you'll never spot a potential artist, designer or

architect by his explosive personality or his far-away look. Toss aside the myth of artistic temperament. There are more concrete signs to watch for, more significant questions that the potential artist should ask himself. Here are some questions you should think about.

How much do you see?

Old friends of Picasso say that when he looked at a painting, they were amazed to find any paint left on the canvas. He seemed to devour things with his eyes.

One striking thing about artists is that they literally *see more intensely* than other people. They watch everything, notice everything: how people dress, how they decorate their homes, how food is arranged on a plate. They often see things other people don't see at all. They discover rich colors in "gray" shadows and may find the subtle shape of a dusty pebble as beautiful as the shining facets of a diamond.

Artists *react strongly* to what they see. Laymen are often baffled by the excitement an artist may find in the tilt of a tree or a slight color change in the sky. My designer friends are literally angry when they see an ugly piece of furniture or an ugly building going up.

You *can* learn to see as an artist sees. This eye can be cultivated, and a good artist's eye becomes sharper every year. No psychologist or geneticist has ever proven that babies are *born* with the artist's eye. In many people, however, the artist's eye seems to develop almost by itself, when they're quite young. This can be an important sign of things to come.

What do you do with your hands?

Artists want to do more than just watch. They feel a powerful urge to do something about what they see, something with their hands.

To an artist, a memorable face is more than something to look at. It's something to draw, paint, sculpt, photograph. When a designer is dissatisfied with a chair he's bought, he's likely to haul out his tools and rebuild it.

I know one designer who's forever rebuilding every stick of furniture in his home. Like most good designers, he's never satisfied. He always has a new idea for improving his surroundings. He's never forgotten the afternoon he brought his future wife home to meet his parents. She was a pianist. Naturally, she was asked to play. The unlucky girl selected a sonata that began with a thunderous series of chords. As her fingers struck the keyboard, the piano collapsed like a load of lumber falling off a truck. Her future husband had been experimenting with a new kind of piano leg. The experiment hadn't worked.

Looking back on high school, I recall many future artists, designers, and architects who had similar obsessions. My friends and I drew constantly, not only in art classes, but in every spare minute we had. The margins of our notebooks were crammed with little sketches of teachers, classmates, an idea for a painting or a school poster. Others among us always seemed to be building things. Their rooms at home bulged with ship and plane models, wood carvings, weird furniture, dioramas, kites, and unfinished constructions that nobody could identify.

Not every artist has this sort of one track mind. Many have diverse interests like music, writing, sports, gardening. Nor does every artist discover his vocation as early as high school. I know several outstanding artists, designers, and architects who were mature men—successful in jobs that had nothing to do with art—before they recognized their true vocation.

But whenever it comes, however it comes, the urge to be an artist implies an urge to work with your hands. You must *like* to work with your hands if you hope to be an artist.

Do you like hard work?

A well known watercolorist was painting outdoors one day when he heard footsteps behind him. He was working in a cornfield near a major truck route. A huge tank truck had pulled up along the side of the road. The driver had climbed out of the cab and strolled over to watch the painter at work. The trucker had never seen this spectacle before. For ten minutes he stared silently over the artist's shoulder. At last, the trucker tapped him on the arm and asked wonderingly: "Tell me the truth. Would you rather do this than work?"

It comes as a surprise to many people that art *is* work, hard work. True, you become an artist because art is fun. But when you reach art school, you must be prepared to face four or five years of rigorous training. A good art, design or architectural school is as tough as any engineering school. There will be times when you'll work far into the night to get passing grades.

And when you land your first job, you'll soon discover that art is more than the usual 9-to-5 routine. Art demands more of you than many other kinds of work. Your mind must be bubbling with fresh ideas throughout the work day. Your hands will work all day, perhaps into the night. For when ideas are surging in your hand and your hands are racing to give these ideas tangible shape, you can't just turn off this process when the clock strikes. Even when your hands are idle—evenings, holidays, weekends—your work may still revolve in your mind because your work is something you love.

This means that a career in art will demand all the energy and dedication you can muster. You don't just *put in* your eight hours like a clerk-typist in the army. You must give all you have, all the time. To live the life of a successful artist, designer or architect, you have to *relish* work and come back for more when someone else would be tempted to go home and lie down. Though *Sunday painting* may look easy, there's nothing soft about the life of the professional artist. The more you love what you do, the harder you're going to work.

Are you adventurous?

One of America's best graphic designers has a unique way of testing his students to separate the sheep from the goats. Each year, he takes his seniors to a fine, though inexpensive, little French restaurant to celebrate their graduation. Some of his students always try to order hamburgers. These, he says, are the ones who are doomed to be second-raters. Others stick their necks out and order the unfamiliar dishes on the menu. Their teacher predicts: "These are the ones to watch."

This is hardly an infallible test, but it does spotlight an important characteristic that most good artists seem to have: they approach life with a spirit of adventure. They're never satisfied with the status quo. They're hungry for new, refreshing experiences.

Most of my friends are constantly combing art galleries, museums, books, magazines, movies, TV shows, the theater, trade exhibits, even department store counters, for new ideas. They're travel hungry. When they finally save up the money for a trip abroad, they don't stay at the fashionable hotel where the help speaks English. The artists pick the little hotel on a side street, where they'll be forced to learn a new language.

Artists are always experimenting. When a new plastic becomes available, industrial designers rush to try it. When a new type face is stocked by typographers and printers, graphic designers are impatient to use it in a layout. It's been said that a true architect might try building with old newspapers if he thought they'd stand up when it rained.

Art is no place for the stick-in-the-mud. There's no room for the man who turns his back on the unfamiliar and insists: "I like what I'm used to."

Do you like to work alone?

Whether he works in the silence of an attic studio or in a bustling office, an artist spends much of his professional life alone.

The painter, sculptor, and printmaker are almost always alone with their thoughts. Some sculptors and mural painters have assistants, and there are models, of course. But fine art is essentially a one man job.

What about the graphic designer in an advertising agency, the illustrator in an art service, the draftsman in an architectural office, and all the other artists who work as members of a team? Even in a team job, the artist is on his own much of the time.

When client meetings and office bull sessions are over, when the work has been scheduled and each man has been given his part of the project, each member of the team returns to his drawing board. If he has a door, he closes it. If his drawing board is in the bullpen with a dozen other boards, he puts up imaginary walls and shuts an imaginary door. He may open that door to ask a question, give an order or take one. But he's on his own till his part of the job is done.

To work on your own—whether in your own studio or "alone" among others—takes some rare qualities. You must have an unusual amount of self-discipline. You have no supervisor standing over you, directing you, making sure you keep at it. It's entirely up to you to get the job done. You must be able to organize your energies, pace yourself, and "keep your eye on the ball." Can you resist the temptation to dawdle, stare out the window, go out for a Coke, make just one more phone call? Can you work steadily, not in fits and starts, but with a smooth, controlled rhythm, like a good long distance runner?

Obviously, such self-discipline is impossible unless you have exceptional ability to concentrate. Artists are often accused of absent mindedness. Their wives complain, "You never hear the doorbell," or "You never look at your watch and that's why you don't get home on time." My particular vice is to nod when people talk to me, but never hear a word they say. This behavior may be irritating, but *absent mindedness* is the wrong word. The artist's mind is very much there. But his mind is so intent on his work that he's closed the door to everything else.

An outstanding fabric designer put it this way: "A real artist has a kind of filter built into his head. It filters out all distractions—voices, noises, invitations, TV—that might take him away from his work." Of course, this isn't *always* true. Though artists who work in offices must develop a knack for ignoring the chaos around them, there are others—many painters, sculptors, free lance illustrators—who can get nothing done unless they retreat to a lonely barn in the country. But one thing is true of *all* these artists. They know how to cut themselves off from the outside world. They're amazingly single minded. When they have a job to do, they focus their minds on that job, nothing else.

All this suggests that an artist must enjoy his own company. You may ask, "Doesn't *everybody* enjoy his own company?" On the contrary, most people are bored stiff when they're by themselves. Most people's free time is spent *avoiding aloneness*. It's spent getting together with other people, or at least watching the TV set to give the illusion that other people are near.

Though artists are as sociable as most people, they really relish being by themselves. A solitary walk in the woods, along a deserted beach, or through the back streets of a strange city may sound depressing to many people. This is an artist's idea of pleasure. He finds it stimulating to be alone with his thoughts.

Self-discipline, concentration, and pleasure in your own company—you *can* manage to be an artist without these rare qualities. But there's not much chance that you'll be a *first rate* artist without them.

Can you work with people?

Reading the last few paragraphs, you may have spotted a paradox. Artists must like to work by themselves, *but* many artists spend their lives working with people.

A painter, sculptor or printmaker can spend his life in an attic if he chooses—though not many do—but what about architects, interior designers, fabric designers, illustrators, photographers, industrial designers, graphic designers, and all the other artists who have clients, bosses, and co-workers? What about all the painters, sculptors, and printmakers who *don't* live in attics, but make part of their living by teaching?

Most artists must not only like working alone, they must be able to work with people.

Working with people *well* takes as many rare qualities as

working alone. Most important is a spirit of give-and-take. Though you must have the courage to stick up for your convictions, give-and-take means having respect for other people's ideas too. It means the ability to compromise, exchange ideas with others, accept criticism gracefully. Whether you're an architect or designer working in an office, a painter or sculptor teaching in an art school, you must *enjoy* this give-and-take with your co-workers or students.

This really brings us back to the issue of artistic temperament. The spirit of give-and-take is the *opposite* of artistic temperament. At the beginning of this chapter, I said that a stubborn, arrogant, fiery personality was no sign of talent. Now I'll go a step further: so-called artistic temperament is one of the biggest roadblocks a young artist can erect in his own path.

How much do you care about money?

Contrary to legend, most good artists, designers, and architects earn a comfortable living.

With some notable exceptions—everyone seems to know the sad fate of Van Gogh—most of the painters we remember as old masters and not-so-old masters *were* fairly well known in their own day. The architects we remember as great *did* get to put up important buildings. The sculptors we recall as great *did* manage to land commissions for important monuments. In fact, these names *couldn't* have come down to us if patrons hadn't recognized these men, paid for their work, and preserved it for posterity.

Today, with one disturbing exception, most art fields pay surprisingly well. In architecture and industrial design, to cite two examples, beginning salaries compare quite well with the earnings of engineering and other technical school graduates. In fields like graphic and interior design, beginners often take a financial beating, but potential earnings are high. Unfortunately, it's the painters, sculptors, and printmakers—the group known as fine artists—who have a rough time. But there's hope for them in the many teaching jobs open to artists.

Though teachers' salaries are nothing extraordinary, they're getting better and better.

Make no mistake: the art world is intensely competitive and can be cruel to the man who doesn't make the grade. Advertising agencies have their share of disappointed pasteup boys who once aspired to be art directors. Architectural offices are full of middle aged draftsmen who float from job to job, who'll never claim credit for designing a building. And no one can count the number of painters, sculptors, and printmakers who'll never have a one man show.

However, for the artist who has the necessary talent, training, and perseverance, the financial prospects are encouraging. There's not much chance of his getting rich, but neither is he likely to waste away in a garret. He *can* earn a comfortable living, doing the work he loves.

But no one becomes an artist because of the money he hopes to make. He chooses his profession for its own sake. Ask a serious artist what he'd do if he had no financial worries, if some forgotten uncle willed him a thousand acres of Texas real estate bristling with oil wells. He'd think for a moment and then answer: "I guess I'd just go on being an artist."

If money is an important goal in your life, art is certainly not the way to make it. There are much better ways to make big money: become a stockbroker or a sales executive. Even when an artist achieves financial success on a big scale—which happens now and then—he succeeds precisely because he places his art first and money second.

Aptitude tests

In recent years, psychologists have developed various tests designed to help people choose the right career. These are often called aptitude tests or vocational tests. But these terms are too narrow. They give no idea of the scope of a good battery of tests.

Psychologists speak of a *battery* of tests because they normally expect you to take a selected *group* of tests, not just one. A complete battery includes four kinds of tests. First, there are intelligence tests: how well does your mental equipment operate? Second, there are personality tests: what's your psychological makeup? Third, there are interest tests: are your interests, your attitudes, your personal philosophy more like those of artists or some other professional group? Finally, there are aptitude tests: what are your *native* abilities?

Why not just take a few art aptitude tests and skip the rest? Because these few tests can't tell you enough. Few artists or guidance specialists claim that talent can be tested. As one distinguished psychologist put it: "We have no workable definition of artistic talent. Thus, art aptitude tests have no predictive value, just comparative value." That is, they can't tell you if you'll be happy or successful in art. All they can tell is that you have more or less skill, knowledge, or "esthetic judgment" than the others who've taken the test. This leaves out imagination, ambition, and all the other unknowns that determine an artist's future.

A good guidance agency usually recommends that you take many tests that seem to have nothing to do with art. The tester is interested in studying you from many angles. When the battery is completed and scored, he hopes to give you an objective picture of yourself, free of any preconceptions or illusions you may have. The tester won't write you a directive, telling you exactly what to do with your life. His job is to help you take a fresh look at yourself, so you'll be better equipped to solve *your own* problems. The tester will tell you many things you may not know about yourself, then make some recommendations about types of work that will suit you and characteristics you should look for in a job. Equally important, he may confirm some of your own opinions. But, at this point, the problem is back in your lap. With the self-knowledge you've gained from the tests, you're better equipped to answer your own questions.

Who should take these tests? Not everyone needs them, of course. If you know you want to be an artist, but don't know which art field to pick, tests may not help. Your first year or two in art school will be more likely to solve this rather subtle problem. However, if you're trying to decide between two *totally different* fields, like art and engineering, then a battery of tests, administered by a reputable guidance agency, may be a worthwhile investment. If you're not sure whether a series of tests will help you, discuss your vocational problem with the people at the agency. They'll tell you whether they feel your questions can be answered by tests or simply by enrolling in art school.

Where can you find a reputable guidance agency? There's probably a college or university within driving distance of your home. Many of these now have their own guidance services. College and university guidance services are often open to the public. Charges are generally reasonable.

Many states and major cities have publicly supported guidance agencies. Your local YMCA or YMHA may have a guidance service. So may other public agencies. Many churches and synagogues now have guidance facilities. And many enterprising psychologists and educators have set up their own guidance offices.

When you choose a guidance agency, it's important to go on the recommendation of someone whose judgment you can trust. There are far too many fly-by-night agencies, both public and private, springing up these days to capitalize on the "aptitude test boom." Your high school guidance counselor should know the reputable agencies in your area. If your nearby college or university has no guidance office open to the public, the psychology or education department should be able to make a recommendation.

How much do high school grades mean?

Obviously, the grades you get in high school are worth watching. If you get good grades in art, this should encourage you to consider art as a career. Your teacher has probably seen the work of hundreds of art students. He knows many signs that distinguish a future artist from a hobbyist. Grades are his way of rating your skills and your innate ability.

But having been a teacher, I know that no teacher considers himself infallible. The intelligent teacher always has a secret fear that he's flunked a future Matisse or Frank Lloyd Wright. And sometimes it does happen. All of us can name distinguished artists, designers, and architects who did badly in school.

If you're that rare bird, you won't be tempted to give up because of low grades. Your urge to be an artist will be so strong that *nothing* can discourage you. Your teacher *could* be wrong. And he'll be the first to congratulate you when you prove him so.

3
Planning your high school program

Many high schools have just one art teacher. He's a one man department and his time is limited, which means that *you're* limited in the number of art classes you can take. Bigger high schools are often lucky enough to have several art teachers. This may mean that more art classes are open to you. In some large cities, there are high schools with art programs as ambitious as the programs of many art schools.

Whatever the size of your high school's art department, you probably have *some* choice when it comes to the amount and type of art you take. Generally, you also have some choices to make about other subjects, like languages, the sciences, and so-called industrial arts classes, such as woodworking and mechanical drawing. In this chapter, I'll try to make some suggestions about how to plan your high school program. I'll also make some recommendations about extracurricular activities, part-time and summer jobs that provide good experience to back up your high school art studies.

How much art should you take?

If you're absolutely sure you're going on to art school or to a college or university art department after high school, then the answer to this question is "All you can get!" If you're really set on an art career, it's important to sit down with your art teacher, or the head of your high school's art department, to plan a course schedule that will give you the most complete art training the school can provide. But bear in mind that you'll be expected to take a "college preparatory program," which means a limited amount of art and a lot of academic subjects (liberal arts, science, etc.) .

In a small school, you may find yourself taking every art class available. In a bigger school with more art classes, there may be only a certain number of art classes you're *allowed* to take. The school will limit your number of art classes so you'll have time for history, science, mathematics, literature, languages, and other subjects necessary for a well rounded education. Your art department will help you decide *which* art classes are best for you, within the limit set by the school.

However, if you're not certain that you want to be an artist, you can't load up just on art courses. You have to plan a program that lets you experiment with a variety of subjects.

For example, if you're weighing engineering against architecture, you can't expect your high school to have courses in bridge building or the design of small houses. But you *can* take math and physics, basic training for engineers as well as architects. You can also take some classes in drawing and painting, both fundamental to architecture. It may also be wise to take some classes in "shop" or mechanical drawing, which will help you in *either* field. Some schools even teach architectural drafting.

The trick is to find room in a crowded program to experiment with all these subjects. Keep in mind that the teachers in these various departments are there to help you. Don't hesitate to ask their aid in planning a complicated class schedule.

What art subjects are most important?

In a big high school, lucky enough to have several art teachers, you may find that different subjects are taught in different art classes. One class may emphasize drawing and painting, while another may stress crafts like ceramics, metal and leather work.

Which class will be most valuable to a future artist, designer or architect?

Smaller schools rarely have specialized art classes, but one art class often manages to cram in an astonishing variety of subjects. You may get a taste of painting, drawing, sculpture, printmaking, illustration, fabric design, poster design, and art appreciation all in one class. If you have a choice of assignments, which should you pick?

Drawing is first on the list. An artist who can't draw is as unthinkable as an author who can't read and write. Whatever art field you finally choose, drawing is something you must learn at the very beginning.

As you might expect, next on the list comes painting. When you draw, you learn to think in line, light, and shadow. Now, painting reveals the vast possibilities of color and texture. Wherever you go in the art world, you must carry with you the lessons that only painting can teach.

Third is sculpture. When you draw and paint, you work in two dimensions. Sculpture introduces you to the third dimension. This is why many art schools call their sculpture courses *three dimensional design*. Having explored the possibilities of line, light and shade, color and texture, you now face the challenge of building real forms in space.

Finally, nothing is more valuable than a good knowledge of the great art of past and present. Such courses usually go under the heading of art appreciation or art history.

Not a very long list. But if you've studied these four subjects thoroughly, you've had a taste of the fundamental problems you'll meet later in *any* art career. This short list of basic subjects should encourage you if your high school seems too small to offer a broad art program. Even if a school has just one art teacher, he probably teaches these fundamental subjects. Most good art teachers recognize that these four subjects come first.

On the other hand, if your high school—like some big city schools—offers a confusing diversity of art subjects, it helps to keep in mind that just four subjects form the foundation of all art training.

What other art subjects are useful?

Today it's possible to find some high schools teaching interior design, architecture, industrial design, ceramics, photography, book and magazine illustration, printmaking (etching, woodcut, lithography) , graphic design, fabric design, silversmithing, and still other subjects that come under such vague headings as art appreciation and arts and crafts. The list could go on for a page. If you have several of these subjects to choose among, which ones deserve your time?

The value of a subject depends in part on how well it's taught. I once watched a superb teacher of design devote a week to showing his class how to split, whittle, and chop shapes out of bamboo. If any other teacher had scheduled this classroom project, it would have seemed a waste of time. But *he* made "bamboo week" an unforgettable episode in the lives of thirty future designers.

Nevertheless, I think it's possible to make a few generalizations about the comparative value of some common art subjects.

For the purposes of this chapter, it may be helpful to divide high school art subjects into *general* and *pre-professional*. By general, I mean basic subjects that are useful background for any art profession you may finally choose. By pre-professional, I mean subjects that prepare you for later professional training in a specific art field, but may not be useful background for some *other* art career.

If you haven't set your mind on a particular art field, then it's best to stick to subjects in the general category. Beyond the four basics—drawing, painting, sculpture, and art history—there are a number that can be valuable training for any art career.

Printmaking tends to teach the same lessons as drawing and painting. Unhappily, too few schools have etching presses, lithographic presses, and the other necessary equipment. Ceramics can be almost as good training as sculpture, with the added advantage that ceramics will teach you a lot about color. Again there's the trouble that too few schools can afford kilns, potters' wheels, and other equipment. Though illustration might be put in the pre-professional category, it has general value too. After all, illustration is just drawing or painting under another name.

Often a subject is given some vague title like *design* or *visual techniques*. If this means experimentation with color, line, texture, form, and other basic design elements, then this qualifies as good general background.

Now, what's the value of pre-professional subjects like industrial design, fabric design, and the others mentioned at the beginning of this section? Certainly, if you're dead set on being an industrial designer, it pays to take the subject in high school, *if* you can get it. The same holds true for any art profession you're *sure* you want to enter. If you're lucky enough to attend a high school that teaches the subject, take it. It's no substitute for professional training in art school, college or university, but it will help you when you get there.

But let me add one note of caution: you *may* change your mind about the art field you want to enter. Art schools are full of students who have switched majors, even as late as their senior year. This could happen to *you*. If you do change your mind, you'll be grateful for all the general subjects you've taken. Everything you learned from your drawing, painting, sculpture, and art history assignments can be used in your new career field, just as it was in your previous field.

In short, if your high school *does* offer the right pre-professional subject, you should certainly take it. But don't load up on pre-professional classwork at the *expense* of general art subjects. You may regret it.

Are industrial arts subjects worth taking?

Many high schools offer a variety of subjects roughly classed as *industrial arts*. A few of these may be useful to future artists, though in a limited way.

Woodworking, metalworking, and other "shop" subjects can be good experience for the future industrial designer, architect, interior designer, furniture designer, sculptor or any other artist who works in three dimensions. These classes can be a good introduction to the problems of structure and materials.

Drafting, often called mechanical drawing in high school, is a skill no architect, industrial or interior designer can get along without. This is a skill that's worth developing early *if* you're sure you're heading for one of these fields. High school can be a good place to begin.

The point is simply this: take these industrial arts subjects *only* if you're certain you're going into an art field where you can use them. There's no sense in taking metalworking or woodworking, for instance, if you hope to be an illustrator. Above all, don't invest so much time in industrial arts subjects that you neglect your other art classes.

Why are academic subjects necessary?

Earlier in this chapter, I pointed out that most high schools insist that you take a great many classes outside the art department. Most of these are the so-called academic subjects, such as English composition and literature, history, social studies, languages, music appreciation, mathematics, and sciences like biology, chemistry, and physics. Why are these so important?

You'll find the most obvious reason by scanning a few art school catalogs. It's difficult to get into most good art schools, colleges, and universities without a reasonable number of academic subjects on your high school record.

But this isn't the only reason. A noted consultant in the interiors field once put it this way: "Take two young men of equal talent and equal art training. The one with the richer education in the liberal arts and the sciences will automatically go ahead faster."

The artist with the *liberal education* knows more about more things. His curiosity reaches out in more directions. He reads more and gets more out of what he reads. He expresses himself more effectively, in writing or in conversation. He's like an athlete who's built up *all* his muscles, not just a few. This is why a good high school expects you to be more than a good *art* student. The high school's job isn't to train artists, but rather to build a *whole man*.

What extracurricular activities are good experience?

High school is more than classwork. All sorts of extracurricular activities can be part of your high school art training. These are good experience and they're a good thing to have on your record when you apply for admission to art school.

High schools need posters, advertising everything from a dance to fire drill instructions. A poster is a good basic graphic design problem. Doing the lettering may be your introduction to typography. If the poster carries a picture, this can be a stimulating job for a future illustrator.

School publications—newspapers, magazines, yearbooks— often need illustrations too. And with the exception of the newspaper, traditionally "made up" by the editors, some future graphic designer must lay out all these pages before they go to the printer.

Stage sets for school plays demand the services of artists and designers. Backdrops are paintings on a vast scale. Designing a set that's practical, durable, handsome, and easy to build—something that actors can really live with while they're on stage—can be fine experience for a future architect, industrial or interior designer. The same holds true for the many exhibits that are designed and built in high schools each semester, another opportunity for the future architect and designer.

Every high school presents different opportunities. Is there a dance for which you can paint, carve, or construct decorations? Does the school need murals, reliefs, banners, new stationery? Is there a parade for which you can design floats? This is a good job for a future sculptor. These are all opportunities you should watch for. And there are many more.

What if your high school art program is too limited?

Not all high schools have adequate art programs. *Some have no art teacher at all.* Others may share an art teacher with neighboring schools. Still others may have one or more art teachers, but have such crowded classes that you can't get enough personal attention. What can you do if you can't get enough art in your high school?

If your high school doesn't have a full-time art teacher, ask your advisor or your principal if it's possible to transfer to a nearby school that has a more ambitious art program. You may have to get up early in the morning and do some heavy commuting, but it might be worth the trouble.

If your art classes are crowded and you can't get enough of your teacher's time, your fellow students and your overworked art teacher may be just as frustrated as you are. If there are *enough* art majors to back you up, you may be able to get the school to hire an additional art teacher. Your present teacher may be delighted to get some help. Discuss the idea with him, your principal, the Parent-Teachers Association, and the school board.

Naturally, these suggestions may turn out to be impractical. In that case, you have to go outside the school for supplementary art training. Is there an art school within commuting distance? Many art schools now offer evening and weekend classes. Is there a local artist who teaches a private class in his studio? Your high school art teacher might be able to recommend someone.

What if you can't afford outside art classes? What if there's no art school nearby? Many outstanding artists have been self-taught, at least in their early years. Buy whatever art materials you can afford and devote all the time you can spare to painting, drawing, and sculpture. You'll be amazed at how much you can learn on your own, by hard, steady work. We're told that Giotto, the first great artist of the Renaissance, was a shepherd boy who taught himself to draw with a stick in the dirt.

Your local library or bookstore can be a fair substitute for an art school. An extraordinary number of good art textbooks are now available. Distinguished art teachers have put their knowledge into print. If you *must* work on your own, these books are the next best thing to having a teacher at your elbow.

Must you major in art?

It's not uncommon for a high school student to decide on an

art career in his senior year or even after graduation. By then, it's too late to switch to an art major. How can you catch up with your fellow students who *were* art majors?

As I explained a moment ago, you can still take some courses in a nearby art school. Or you can work independently, with the aid of some good art instruction books. Even if graduation is already past, there may still be time to take a summer course in art school or spend the summer working on your own.

Since time is short, it's wisest to concentrate on drawing and painting. Sculpture is a slow process, too slow if you're embarking on a "crash program" to prepare for art school in the fall. Better put that off until you're in art school.

But what if you didn't major in art and circumstances have prevented spare-time study? What are your odds of getting into a good art school? Don't be discouraged. Many of the best art schools, colleges, and universities will give you a chance to prove yourself. This is one purpose of the foundation year that begins many art school programs.

4
Choosing an art school

The dean of a well known art school was talking to a little boy enrolled in the Saturday morning classes for children. "What made you come here?" the dean asked. The little fellow pondered the question for a moment. At last, he seemed to hit on the reason: "It smells better than the zoo."

Many mature artists look back to find that they picked their schools for reasons that weren't much better. A famed advertising art director worked as a farm laborer in his teens, saved just enough money for a year in art school, then hitchhiked 2000 miles to an obscure school whose ad caught his eye in a magazine. A noted illustrator picked her college because "the girls seemed so well dressed." A successful interior designer picked the university with the most picturesque campus: "I was impressed by the groves of trees and the ivy on the walls."

Choosing your art school, college or university isn't that simple. You're investing years of your life and thousands of dollars. This isn't all that's at stake. Your professional future depends, in part, on your professional training. The wrong school can do damage that takes years to repair, *if* the damage can be repaired.

There are more bad schools than good. How do you pick a *good* school out of the hundreds that advertise, get listed in school directories, and mail catalogs to all comers? How can a teenager and his family—whose only contact with the complex art world has been the local high school—hope to make the right choice?

Where to go for information

Don't rely on your hunches. Don't rely on the so-called reputation of a particular school: reputations are often undeserved.
When you finally settle on a school, your decision should be
based on thorough, hard-headed research. This research isn't
hard to do. Here are some suggestions about where to go for
facts and opinions.

A logical place to begin is your high school. Your art teacher
is often familiar with the art schools, colleges, and universities
nearby. He may not know them all, but he's probably had students who went on to these schools and reported back. He himself may be a graduate of a local school. Over the years, he's
probably gathered plenty of pros and cons. If he's willing to
recommend a school, his judgment is worth noting.

You should also talk to your high school's guidance counselor,
sometimes called the college advisor. He won't claim to be an
art expert, but like your art teacher, he's probably heard the
reports of students who've gone on to various art schools, colleges, and universities. It's also his job to know something about
the admission requirements, programs, facilities, and costs of
these schools. He has stacks of catalogs and reference books with
this data. If he doesn't have *all* the facts on hand, he'll know
where to find more.

You should certainly try to meet graduates of the schools
you're investigating. Your high school teacher and guidance
counselor may know some who live nearby. As a matter of fact,
there may be many local artists, designers, and architects who
are worth meeting, whatever school they attended. A mutual
friend or your high school art teacher might arrange an introduction. If there's no mutual friend to introduce you, I see no
harm in getting the names of some professionals in the neighborhood and writing them a note. Not all of them will have
time to see you. But you may be surprised how many busy men
are willing to spend a few minutes advising young people. Even
if they can spare just fifteen minutes, that conversation can mean
a lot.

Obviously, you should try to visit the schools themselves.

There can be no substitute for a first hand look at faculty, students, facilities, and student work. Write or phone ahead for an appointment. There may be special visitors' days. When you arrive, don't be shy about bombarding faculty members with questions.

School catalogs come *last* on my list of information sources. Write for the catalog of every school that interests you. It will usually be mailed to you without charge. Catalogs contain useful data about faculty, course lists, admission and graduation requirements, deadline dates and calendars of events, descriptions of facilities, plus a lot more.

But many catalogs are meant to do more than inform. Their job is to advertise, to *sell* you. The photos naturally show the well equipped studios and ignore the badly equipped workrooms elsewhere in the school. When "typical student work" is illustrated, it's far from typical. The rare examples of outstanding student work are shown. The text spotlights famous faculty members, though there's no reason to believe that celebrities make better teachers than lesser known men.

I must emphasize that I see nothing wrong with a catalog that tries to sell you. A school has every right to put its best foot forward. Nobody expects a catalog to show dingy classrooms and crude student work. But as you read a catalog, you must do your best to separate facts from sales talk.

Actually, catalogs that avoid sales talk are often worse. Year after year, an appalling number of schools issue catalogs that neither advertise *nor* inform. Many excellent schools have catalogs that are tastelessly designed, shabbily printed, haphazardly organized, and ponderously written. Few readers can wade through this morass of bureaucratic gobbledygook. Facts may be even *less* accessible than the facts in the sales talk catalog.

If some schools' catalogs are obviously designed to lure you, many others seem designed to drive you away. This simply proves you can't take a catalog at face value. Handsome publications don't necessarily come from good schools. Nor do shoddy publications always represent bad schools. Get lots of catalogs, read them as carefully as your patience allows, but don't pick or reject a school on the basis of its printed matter.

A catalog is just one more source of information. It can answer some questions, but not others.

A checklist of questions you should ask

You can talk to all the people I've listed, read catalogs from cover to cover, but still end up knowing very little. It's too easy for people to tell you about schools in general terms, exchange pleasantries, and get way off the subject. You go home wondering what the conversation was all about. Reading can be just as useless. After you've read a few catalogs, they all begin to sound alike. Your head bulges with facts, but they don't line up in any useful order. They're just one big blur.

This won't happen if you know what facts you're looking for. You must plan your conversations as carefully as a newspaper reporter plans an interview with a busy celebrity who can spare just fifteen minutes. Nobody will resent it if you write your questions down in advance and show up with a little book to take notes. People will probably be flattered. It may also be helpful to keep certain questions in mind and take notes as you read a catalog. Or you may find it simplest to mark up the catalog with a red pencil as you read.

It's best to start out with a basic list of questions you'd like answered. You won't ask everyone *all* the questions, just the questions you think he can answer. You'll also find that unexpected questions, not on your list, will pop up as the conversation moves along. However, there are fourteen questions I'd like to suggest as your basic list. Though you may want to add some questions of your own, these fourteen represent the essential facts you need to know about any art school, college or university art department.

(1) How long is the school's program?

Most art educators have found that it takes at least four years to train an artist, designer or architect. A few top art schools manage to do a good job in three, but most leading schools have standardized on four. Colleges and universities almost always have four year programs. Subjects like architecture and industrial design often take five in a university.

Steer clear of art schools that offer shortcuts and promise "quick results" like some patent medicine.

One of the first things you should check in a school catalog is the length of the program. Keep in mind that a four year program usually leads to a degree or some sort of certificate. In some art fields, degrees are vital. Part Two of this book—the chapters that deal with the various art professions—will tell you the fields in which degrees count. Keep in mind, too, that many schools allow you to get a degree in three years, *if* you attend summer classes.

(2) What majors are offered?

Many leading schools offer a separate professional program in each art field. There may be a distinct program, perhaps offered by a special department, in any of the major fields dealt with in this book: painting, sculpture, printmaking, illustration, graphic design, fabric design, interior design, architecture, industrial design, photography or art teaching.

Other schools offer just one program, usually called a general art major. This includes a bit of everything. The student can often take one or two courses in *any* of the fields I've listed. In a few fields—particularly fine arts subjects like painting and drawing—there may be several classes open.

A third type of art program is really a compromise between the general art major and the specialized professional program. This is called a general art major with *areas of concentration*. You still take a bit of everything, but you also pick one or two art fields in which you take all the courses you can get.

Finally, there are highly specialized schools that teach just one subject, like painting or photography.

Which kind of school is best? I'd choose the school that offers a separate professional program in each art field. Or I'd pick the school that offers a general art major with areas of concentration, provided I could take *a lot* of courses in my special field. Unfortunately, many schools *claim* to offer areas of concentration within the general art major, but this often means nothing more than a couple of extra courses.

Without a real area of concentration—a solid block of specialized courses—the general art major just doesn't qualify as professional training. After four years, you discover that you know a little about lots of things, but you're not really a professional in any single art field. When the time comes to land a job, you'll find it hard to complete with graduates who majored or concentrated in a specific art profession.

My objection to the one-subject school is quite different. Actually, a highly specialized school often does an excellent teaching job just because it concentrates on one subject. But you have to be mighty sure you want to be an interior designer, for example, before you enroll in a school that teaches nothing but interior design. Few students have picked their art field before they enter art school They know they want to be some sort of artist, but they haven't settled on a particular art profession yet. It takes a year or two of experimentation, maybe more, to find out. Even when the student at last feels sure, he often changes his mind. In the one-subject school, you obviously can't experiment with several art fields. Nor can you switch your major or shift your area of concentration if your professional interests change.

What about teachers' colleges, where you can only study art teaching? Aren't *these* one-subject schools? As you'll find when you read Chapter 13 on art teaching, a good teachers' college actually offers the equivalent of a general art major. Furthermore, the best teachers' colleges encourage you to concentrate in one or more art fields.

A school's catalog will tell you what majors or areas of concentration are offered. It should also specify what courses are available in your area of concentration. If the catalog is unclear, ask when you visit the school.

(3) How flexible is the program?

Contact with many art fields is an essential part of your education. Though I've stressed the importance of specialization, you *should* have the freedom to take courses in many fields outside your major or your area of concentration. Good schools often insist that you *elect* several art classes from a list of subjects distantly related to your major.

Unhappily, there's one notable exception to this rule. Architectural programs are often rigidly separated from other art programs. In many universities, the architectural school is kept entirely divorced from the art or design school, and the two have amazingly little contact. The architects have made this decision, and I think architectural training has been severely damaged by the separation. The most you can do is pick an architectural school that will allow you some slight freedom to take courses in other art fields.

A school's catalog will probably list *electives* along with required courses. Again, if the catalog is unclear, you can check when you visit the school.

(4) Does the program begin with a foundation year?

Most good art programs begin with what educators call a *foundation year,* a year of basic training. This includes fundamentals like drawing, painting, sculpture, printmaking, design in two and three dimensions, and art history. You have no major subject this first year. Or if you do have a major in a specific art field, you take only a few classes in this field. Most foundation year courses are required: they're the same whatever your major or your area of concentration.

This year of basic training has two purposes. It builds up your muscles for the more advanced courses you'll face in the years ahead. And equally important, this exploratory year helps you get to know yourself better in preparation for choosing a major or an area of concentration.

The school catalog will tell you whether there's a foundation year. Remember that it doesn't *have* to be called the foundation year. It might be called the *orientation year* or have no name at all. The thing to look for is a list of first year required courses: basic subjects which all students must take.

When you visit the school, you can get more details about the first year course list. Alumni of the school can also supply details.

(5) How much emphasis is placed on fine art?

Just as your year of basic training emphasizes the fine art subjects on which all art is based—drawing, painting, sculpture, printmaking—your advanced years should include some of these too. If you major in a fine art field, of course, you'll be able to take a great many. But you should continue to absorb these fundamentals no matter what your major.

After the foundation year, many schools continue to *require* fine art courses in succeeding years. If not, the school may arrange your program with gaps for *elective* fine art courses. In the latter case, the choice is left up to you. Either way is good.

Check the course lists in the catalog for fine art requirements and electives. You might also discuss this with faculty members and alumni.

(6) Are the advanced courses really professional?

Beyond basic fine art subjects, a school's program must include many specialized, practical, professional courses. These courses must really duplicate—as far as any class can—what you'll be doing for a living when you graduate. Industrial designers should develop and build products that really work, that can be made on a real production line and sold. Graphic designers should create pages that could be sent right down to the printer, ads that could sell real products. Painters, sculptors, and printmakers should be expected to turn out work of exhibition caliber.

These seem like obvious requirements. They're certainly obvious to your future employer, client, agent, or dealer. Yet a surprising number of schools make no attempt to duplicate professional working conditions. Design students, for example, are often starved for practical problems while they mark time in fine art and classes in design theory. These fundamental subjects *are* vital. But devoting *too* much time to such courses is a common dodge: this can be a school's way of covering up its inability to teach *professional* design subjects.

Fine art programs are often *frankly* non-professional. Many painting, drawing, and sculpture classes—particularly in colleges and universities—are given as a form of recreation, like sports or "social dancing." Amateurs and future professionals may work side-by-side in the same classroom. Hobbyists almost always outnumber professionals in these classes, and the instructor is *forced* to devote most of his time to the amateurs.

How can you find out whether a school's program is *really* professional? The catalog won't tell you. Nor will the faculty. You have to ask local artists, designers, and architects who've hired graduates and tested their professional skill. Above all, talk to alumni. After a few years on the job, they'll know how well, or how badly, the school prepared them for a career in the competitive art world.

(7) Are liberal arts and science courses included?

In the previous chapter, I stressed the importance of academic (or liberal arts) subjects in high school—pointing out that the function of high school isn't to train professional artists, but to develop well rounded young men and women. Colleges, universities, and most of our art schools will also expect you to take a fair number of liberal arts and science courses—essential if you want a degree—on the assumption that broadly educated people make the most successful artists, designers, and architects.

Frankly, I think this is a *debatable* assumption. When I was an art school administrator, I believed in the gospel of the *well rounded man* (I was paid to believe in it), but now I have my doubts. Among the hundreds of successful people I've met in the art world, there are plenty who do owe their success to a well rounded education, but there are just as many who went to the top because they had one track minds, with room in their heads for nothing but art. You may be the sort of artist whose creative powers are enriched and invigorated by studying the liberal arts and the sciences; or you may be so absorbed in your art that courses in anything else seem irrelevant and distracting. Whether you have a one track mind or the multi-track mind of the well rounded man, there's room for you in the art world either way.

Unfortunately for the one track mind, our educational system is rigged in favor of the well rounded man. Our college and university programs are dedicated to the concept of a *liberal education* leading to a degree, which means plenty of liberal arts and sciences. And most of our art schools are now patterned after liberal arts colleges.

If you lean toward a broad education—and you definitely want a degree—one advantage of a college or university is that you can take so many more courses in the liberal arts and sciences. Colleges and universities usually teach these subjects better than art schools. An art school often recognizes this and arranges for students to take their academic courses at a nearby college or university. However, some of the bigger art schools now have their own courses in the liberal arts and sciences, taught by full-time faculty members or by teachers borrowed from other institutions.

The subjects are similar to the academic courses taught in high school, though on a more advanced level, of course. You'll be required to take a selection of the following: English composition and speech; literature; history and social sciences; philosophy; mathematics; psychology; sciences like chemistry, physics, geology, biology, astronomy, and others; perhaps a modern foreign language like French, German, Spanish, Italian, Russian. You'll also be expected to take subjects like physical education and hygiene. Depending upon the size of the school, there may be other subjects like political science, American civilization, anthropology, and still more. Check a school's catalog to find out what academics are offered and which are required.

If you dread the idea of taking lots of liberal arts and science courses, you'll face less of this in an art school than in a college or university. In fact, some art schools will let you skip the academic subjects entirely if you wish. You get a degree if you take the academics along with the art; you get a certificate or diploma (but not a degree) if you skip the academics and take only art. But let me repeat that most good art schools do offer degrees, for which you *must* take a certain minimum number of academics.

If you're headed for a degree, be sure you pick a school that gives you a rich selection of academic subjects, provided that your art courses don't play second fiddle. Even if you're taking a degree program under protest—because you must have it for professional reasons—it makes sense to get the most stimulating academic program you can find. You might enjoy it more than you think.

(8) How stiff are the school's standards?

When I asked a friend why he left his teaching job at a large state university, he explained: "Anybody can get into this place and anybody can get a diploma." This, in a nutshell, is what educators mean when they say a school has low standards.

Good schools have stiff admission requirements. They ask for a transcript of your high school record and hope to see good grades on the sheet. They check on your extracurricular activities. They want letters of reference from your teachers and from intelligent people who've known you for years. If you don't measure up, the school sends you a polite rejection note.

Good schools may not be easy to get into, but they're even harder to stay in. They expect you to work hard to maintain passing grades. If you don't, out you go. Nor are good schools satisfied with grades that are *merely* passing. The school may not be able to toss you out, but your faculty advisor may encourage you to drop out or try a new field.

Rugged graduation standards are a moral obligation. A British designer once defined a good art school as "a place that throws you out *for your own good* if your teachers don't think you can earn a living when you graduate." A responsible art teacher knows that he can't honestly accept tuition money from a student who'll never be a professional. The school is cheating this student if they let him stay.

Will a school let you spend four or five years there if you're unfit for an art career? Or will the faculty be honest enough to forget your tuition money and tell you to move on, even if your grades are barely passing? These are painful questions, but you *must* ask them. Ask your high school art teacher. He knows which art schools took his least promising students and which took only the best ones. Alumni will recall whether passing grades were too easy to get. Other local artists, designers, and architects have probably seen recent graduates on job hunts. Ask these professionals whether non-professionals are allowed to graduate and embark on hopeless job campaigns.

(9) How good are the instructors?

Schools like to boast that faculty members are professional artists, designers, and architects, not just teachers. This isn't the only test of a teacher's qualifications, but it's a good one. Art, design, and architecture—like other professions—are hard to teach well unless the instructor spends part of his life *doing* what he teaches. Good schools hire seasoned professionals and give them free time to continue outside work.

But the practicing-artists-make-the-best-teachers line must not be taken *too* seriously. Many fine teachers devote very little time to their art. The best painting teacher I've ever known was a mediocre weekend painter. It was his *students* who became good painters. His art wasn't painting, but teaching. He gave his energy and inspiration to his students and saved none for his paintings.

By the same logic, a first rate professional may be a second rate teacher. He may give all his energy and inspiration to his own work and save none for his students.

Beware of big names. Art schools, colleges, and universities like to list famous people as faculty members or under such vague titles as coordinators, visiting critics, or consultants. Though many of these men do make an important contribution to the school's program, plenty of others just lend their names on the condition that no work is required. If they do show up, it's once a year to give a brief talk or to criticize student portfolios. It's important to find out whether celebrities really turn up in the classroom or just appear in the catalog as window dressing.

Catalogs sometimes carry brief biographies of faculty members. Read these but keep in mind that this is all part of the catalog's sales talk. Alumni and other professionals are the best people to ask about a school's faculty.

(10) Are the school's facilities adequate?

One important reason to visit a school is to see the campus and walk through the classrooms. Arrange your visit well in advance, so there's time to schedule a tour, not just a brief chat.

Examine the classrooms just as you would your future home. Are studios well lit? Plenty of daylight? Plenty of artificial light for dim days? Is there enough room so students aren't jammed together, too close to the model, unable to see over all the shoulders? Is there plenty of air? A stuffy room reeking of turpentine, rubber cement, and fixative is a tough place to work.

Equipment is just as important as surroundings. Do easels and drawing boards look sturdy and professional, not flimsy and makeshift? Do the industrial designers have shops with well kept machinery to build things? Do the graphic designers have real metal type to set, plus a printing press or two? Do photography students have a spacious studio, lots of lights, and a thoroughly equipped darkroom?

What other facilities are there? A large, well stocked library? An art materials store that sells supplies at cut rates? An exhibition gallery where student *and* professional work is shown? An art collection? An audio-visual department, with motion picture, sound, and slide projection equipment? A collection of movies, film strips, and slides?

I won't try to give you a complete checklist of the facilities an ideal school should have. But these few paragraphs should suggest the *sort* of things to watch for.

However, don't expect things to look neat and new. School equipment takes incredible punishment. An easel is covered with dried paint and a book with thumb prints after a few months' use. Much equipment comes second hand, is reconditioned, and kept in working order for a generation of students.

The same holds true for the campus. Don't expect every good school to have bright new steel and glass buildings or ivy covered collegiate gothic. Many great schools are in dingy, tumbledown architectural monstrosities, surrounded by slums. It's what goes on *inside* the buildings that counts.

After you've toured a school, compare impressions with other people. Talk to alumni. They've *lived* in the school. Talk to your high school art teacher and guidance counselor. They may have toured the school recently on a special visitors' day for educators. If not, you might be able to arrange your own visitors' day for a group of students and teachers from your high school. Your teachers' practiced eyes will spot a lot that you might miss.

(11) What extracurricular activities are there?

A good school regards extracurricular activities as part of your training. These activities are carefully planned and encouraged by faculty members, often specially appointed for the purpose.

The *least* important extracurricular affairs are dances, alumni reunions, and sports, which *most* schools have. But what are the activities that relate directly to your professional training? Are there student clubs that hold exhibitions and invite distinguished speakers from various professional fields? Are student committees responsible for school events like forums, film programs, competitions, exhibitions? Do these clubs or committees arrange student tours of artists' studios, designers' and architects' offices? Is there a school magazine or newspaper for which students write and illustrate articles on professional subjects?

Catalogs often list extracurricular activities. Faculty members and alumni can give you details.

(12) Does the school have a placement service?

The climax of your years in school isn't the moment you get your diploma. It's the moment you get your first paycheck. If you can't find work when you graduate, your professional training has been wasted. Recognizing this fact, many leading art schools, colleges, and universities have set up special offices to find work for graduates.

A school's placement service functions something like an employment agency, though of course the service is free. The placement office gets to know potential employers in the community and other parts of the country. At the same time, the office gets to know the students by studying their records, talking to instructors, and interviewing the students themselves. When he has an opening to fill, the employer calls the placement office. The placement director knows where to find the right man or woman for the job. Often it works the other way. When he spots a particularly good student, the placement director may phone an employer out of the blue: "I think you should meet a fellow who's graduating this year. He's the right type for your office."

Frequently a school's placement method is more informal, though it may be just as good. Individual faculty members are expected to keep in touch with potential employers. When an employer has an opening, he calls the instructor, who selects candidates from his classes. Even schools that *have* formal placement procedures often rely on these informal methods too.

It's important for a school to have a placement service of *some* sort, formal or informal, so that students aren't just handed a diploma and flung out into the world.

A good placement office may also get part-time and summer jobs for students. A few visionary schools (*too* few) have so-called *cooperative programs*—alternating periods of study and on-the-job training—and this is also the responsibility of the placement office.

If a school has a placement office, the catalog usually says so. But it won't say how active or effective the service is. Nor will the catalog say how much informal placement is done through the faculty. Ask about placement when you visit the school. It's even more revealing to ask alumni who may or *may not* have gotten jobs through the school. You might also talk to local artists, designers, and architects who may recruit talent from the school. They'll know how well the service works for the *employer*.

(13) Where do graduates find work?

Where do graduates find their first jobs and where do they go from there? This double barreled question is the ultimate test of a school.

Every school, even the worst, can point to a few alumni who've made their mark in the world. I know one mediocre art school that continues to boast about a world-famous painter who spent a few weeks there thirty years ago. A few famous names mean nothing. Where do the *bulk* of the students go from school? Can the school honestly say that graduates in the top half of their class can expect *good* jobs? Can the faculty honestly claim that the others—except for the *just passing* students who weren't wise enough to drop out—get *decent* jobs? How many don't find jobs at all?

No school catalog dares to answer these questions unless the placement record is unusually good. Nor can you count on faculty members for a straight answer unless the record is really impressive. You must ask the alumni and the local artists, designers, and architects who employ them.

(14) Is the school accredited?

In each part of the country, educators have set up accrediting groups that rate local colleges and universities. When a school asks to be accredited, the group sends in a team of investigators to examine the faculty, courses, facilities, and standards. If the school passes this rigorous examination, the catalog proudly announces accredition. Most good colleges and universities are accredited by these regional groups.

Many art schools now grant degrees and aspire to the status of colleges; a number of these have won accreditation from groups that accredit colleges and universities. Most—but not *all*—good art schools are accredited by the National Association of Schools of Art. In choosing an architectural school, be sure to look for the stamp of approval of the National Architectural Accrediting Board.

For an *art school*, how important is accreditation really? If an art school meets the requirements listed in this chapter, don't turn up your nose because its catalog doesn't carry the stamp of the regional accrediting body. On the other hand, if an art school *is* accredited, this is one more argument in the school's favor.

When picking a *college* or *university*, accreditation really counts. But remember that accreditation is no *guarantee* that a college or university can turn out a professional artist. The school may still do an inferior job in the complex field of art. When the time comes to select a school, you must do *your own* accrediting. That's what this chapter is for.

An exception: fine art

Having argued so fiercely for a formal, well planned art education, I think it's important to name one artist who's an exception: the fine artist. Many of our best painters, sculptors, and printmakers have had the most *informal* sort of training or no training at all.

Though architects and designers normally spend four or five

years in one school, the fine artist often wanders from one school to another, from one private teacher to another or simply works on his own. He follows his instincts and works out his own curriculum as he goes along. His discipline isn't imposed by a school, but comes from within himself.

For many noted painters, sculptors, and printmakers, this informal kind of education has worked well. If the fine artist chooses his teachers wisely, he can tailor his education to fit him as precisely as a custom made suit. But he's taking a chance. If he makes the wrong choices, he can do himself real harm. If he lacks self-discipline, there's no school program to impose discipline: like too many art students, he can waste years coasting through various schools and private classes, without ever being nailed down to serious work.

So then, there *are* some valid reasons for formal training even in fine art. By long trial-and-error, a good school has developed a program that fits most students reasonably well. The school knows that this program won't fit every student perfectly, so your course schedule is usually flexible enough to let you experiment with various instructors and subjects. With the advice of your teachers, you *are* encouraged to make many of your own decisions. For every successful fine artist who followed his hunches and wandered from school to school, there's another who voted for formal training and spent his years in *one* school.

And don't overlook one other argument, and a powerful one, for formal training. The next chapter will tell you that few fine artists make a living at painting, sculpture, or printmaking. For most of them, teaching jobs are the main source of income. Many of the best teaching jobs demand a degree, which means at least four years of formal training.

A word about small colleges

The fourteen point checklist you've just read eliminates many small colleges. Often the best liberal arts and teachers' colleges are just too small to have the full scale professional program advocated in this chapter. Does this mean that a future artist, designer, or architect should steer away from small colleges?

On the contrary, a good small college is a splendid choice *if* you recognize the purpose of such a school. Liberal arts colleges—plus the many teachers' colleges now set up on similar lines—educate the *whole man*. Their purpose is to provide a broad education in the liberal arts and the sciences, the kind of education that builds a solid intellectual foundation for any profession you may choose.

Many talented artists, designers, and architects go to a small college first, take all the art they can, along with all their other courses, *then* go to art school for real professional training. Several top art schools have special two year programs for college graduates. Other art schools will arrange special programs on request. This combination of college and art school takes time, but I'm tempted to say that this is the ideal training for a future artist if he can afford it.

The role of the small art school

My fourteen point checklist also seems to eliminate the small art school and the private class. Yet it's certainly true that many of our best artists have gone to schools with just two or three faculty members working in a loft on some side street. Others have studied with an artist in his studio and never gone to school at all. Just what can the small school or private class contribute?

I've already pointed out that *fine art* training can be quite informal. Many of the greatest names in painting, sculpture, and printmaking conduct private classes or teach in schools too small to have a formal program or grant a degree.

A small school may also be particularly good if the teachers stick to just one subject like photography or fashion illustration. This sort of school might also be useful for a limited, rather technical subject like drafting or photo-retouching.

A private class or a small school may also be an exciting *supplement* to the program of a bigger school. If you're majoring in fabric design at a big, four year school, you may still want the inspiration of working Saturdays or summers in the private class of a noted weaver.

If your formal training is behind you and you want to switch fields, a few courses in a small, specialized school may be all you need to add the necessary background. For example, if you're an illustrator who wants to move into the related field of graphic design, all you may need are a few classes in layout and typography. A small school or private class may also be an ideal place for a refresher course in some half-forgotten subject.

What most small schools are *not* good for is the comprehensive professional program on which most art careers are built. Such schools have neither the staff nor the facilities to do a job this big.

Evening and Saturday classes

Many art schools, college and university art departments offer professional programs in the evening or on Saturdays. Such part-time programs are planned for students who work during the day. These courses may lead to some sort of certificate or even to a degree.

Part-time training has some obvious drawbacks, but also some advantages that are often overlooked. The most conspicuous drawback is simply that part-time education takes so terribly long. If full-time training takes four years, equivalent work in evening and Saturday classes may take twice that long. A school's usual solution is to offer a stripped down version of the daytime program. At its best, this is a really concentrated series of courses, an intensive professional program for people who are willing to work *harder* than day students. At its worst, this often turns out to be a superficial program, covering less territory in less detail.

But there are also real advantages in evening and Saturday classes. If you're working at an art job of some kind during the day, and attending art school at night, your lessons may seem far more real than they do to the full-time student who's never really worked at art professionally. You apply by day what you learn at night. Another advantage of evening and Saturday classes is that you sometimes get better teachers than during the day. Many top professionals can't spare the time to teach during the day, but they *can* teach after hours.

Should you work during the day and go to school part-time? Yes, but only if you *must*. If you can afford four or five years of full-time training, you'll have more fun, be less exhausted, and probably get a more complete education. But if you have to earn money during the day, part-time training is your only way of becoming an artist. Pick your part-time school as carefully as you'd pick a full-time school. The same fourteen questions apply.

A final warning about choosing a school

Art is a profession. Like all professions, art demands long, hard, and well organized training. But few art schools, college or university art departments can meet the professional standards set forth in these pages.

Unlucky students pay the price. Each year, thousands of would-be artists finish school and begin pounding the pavements looking for jobs, free lance assignments, one man shows. They've been led to believe they're professionals, destined to move ahead in a glamorous and rewarding field. But too few really have the talent or training to survive in the fierce competition of the art world. For each graduate of professional caliber, there are others who'll take dead end jobs if they can get them, stay there, or drop out of the field altogether.

Week after week, employers see the crude portfolios and hopeful faces of the beginners who won't make the grade.

There are the students who've spent a year or two in some fly-by-night school, taking a few painting and drawing classes, plus a few courses in some vague subject called commercial art. All they have to show for their money are some battered oil paintings, imitation *Saturday Evening Post* covers, a few dog-eared charcoal sketches, and a couple of examples of photo-retouching.

There are graduates of bigger, better known art schools who should never have gotten a diploma. Maybe the school couldn't afford to refuse their tuition money. Maybe the instructors never had the courage to flunk them out or advise them to leave. Whatever the reason, these unlucky students are in the wrong field and no one has had the guts to tell them.

There are college and university graduates who took an art major without realizing that they weren't really enrolled in a professional program. Their teachers had never really decided whether the program was meant to train real artists or simply "raise the cultural level of the students." There were many courses that were *almost* professional, but not quite, a lot of classes in a lot of subjects, but not enough in *any single* subject. The misguided graduate walks the streets with his portfolio and is stunned to discover that he's not equipped to hold down a job in *any* art field. He's not even sure which art field he wants.

Most painful are the job hunters who have obvious talent but chose the wrong school. Too often, the wrong school is a large, widely publicized art school, college, or university that fails to live up to its reputation. In the *right* school, his talent would have blossomed. But he chose his school by its *name*, not by its performance, and his talent has been allowed to stagnate. After four years, he's still an amateur and may remain an amateur for life. He *knows* he's good—or could be— and wonders why no one offers him a job.

These young people have been cheated. Their teachers have permitted them to invest money, time, and hope in a worthless education. It takes a long, depressing job hunt to reveal the grim truth. Some of the talented ones will make it in spite of their inadequate training. They'll teach *themselves* or go back to school, a good school this time. But others, perhaps just as talented, will be permanently maimed. And God knows what happens to all those whose barely passing grades encouraged them to stay in a profession where they don't belong!

Choosing the right school is far from easy. Few art schools, college or university art departments can give satisfactory answers to all fourteen questions in the checklist you've just read. But you must insist that a school give *reasonable* answers to *most* of them. Your professional future depends on these answers.

Choosing your major subject in art school

Having picked your school, your next problem is to pick the art subject you plan to major in, or the subject you'll choose for your area of concentration if you're taking a general art major.

For most students, this is a difficult choice. There's so much you need to know about each field before you can decide. What sort of work do you actually do in a particular art field? What must you study to prepare for the job? What's a typical first job like? What will later jobs be like?

As I've already pointed out, your first year of art training, the *foundation year*, is planned to give you a taste of many kinds of work. However, the foundation year can't answer *all* your questions. Its main purpose is to help you get to know yourself—your skills and your leanings—so that you can answer *your own* questions. Just as you did when you picked a school, you have to do some research. Talk to students in advanced classes—they've already picked their majors—and ask what their classes are like. Attend lectures by visiting professionals and fire questions at them. Talk to your teachers and to every professional who's willing to share his knowledge with you.

The chapters that follow are meant to help you in your fact-finding. Each of these chapters presents a thumbnail sketch of a major art field. For each field, I'll try to answer the basic questions most students have on their minds. As you read these chapters, compare one art career with another and measure yourself against all of them. Just where do your personality, interests, and abilities seem to fit?

Part Two
Choosing a Career

5
Fine art

The Mexican muralist, Diego Rivera, rarely worked outdoors.
But one afternoon, a peasant discovered Rivera in a field, working on an immense canvas. The canvas was covered with daubs
of color. Even more color was piled on the small wooden
palette in the artist's hand. For ten minutes, the peasant
watched Rivera's brush flash from palette to canvas, then from
canvas back to palette. The artist turned and asked, "What
do you think?" The peasant replied solemnly, "It is very
beautiful. But tell me, do you take the colors from the piece
of wood and put them on the canvas, or do you take them from
the canvas and put them on the piece of wood?"

   The story contains a lesson. If you plan to devote your life
to fine art—painting, drawing, sculpture, printmaking—be prepared for lots of public curiosity, but not much understanding.
It takes real courage to become a fine artist. This is the toughest
of all art careers.

What is fine art?

Most teenagers begin as fine artists. They draw, paint, carve
wood, model clay. They do this for no "practical" purpose, just
for the joy of expressing themselves. Perhaps this is the simplest
way to explain the phrase *fine art*, in contrast with what is
sometimes called *useful* or *applied* art. Fine art—a drawing,

painting, sculpture, or print—is an end in itself. You hang it on a wall or set it on a pedestal and there it stands. Unlike applied art—a building, a fabric, or a piece of furniture—fine art has no job to do. Its only function is to be looked at and enjoyed.

By the time they reach art school, many teen-age fine artists decide to channel their skills into the applied arts. The young painter may become an illustrator or graphic designer. The young sculptor may turn to architecture or industrial design. But despite parents' and teachers' warnings to "be practical," a surprising number of young people make the courageous decision to stay in fine art.

Can a fine artist earn a living?

If you plan to devote your life to painting, drawing, sculpture, or printmaking, there's one unpleasant fact you *must* face. You can't count on earning a living by the sale of your work.

Many surveys have been conducted among the nation's fine artists to find out how they make a living. Inevitably, the researchers find that most artists depend on sales for only a small part of their income. As a painter friend of mine put it, "When you sell a picture, it's like finding money in the street: great when it happens, but you can never count on it."

Most fine artists rely on some other source for the bulk of their income. For many artists, this source is a teaching job. Painters and printmakers often do free lance illustration or graphic design; or they hold down steady jobs in these fields. There are sculptors who design furniture and painters who design fabrics. And there are many fine artists who make their living at something totally unrelated to art. Among the best artists I know are an engineer, a lawyer, a dentist, a writer, two actors, and a beautician.

You may ask: "What about the really big name artists, the ones who exhibit at big New York galleries, get into museum collections, and get written up in art magazines? Don't *they* live by selling their work?"

The unhappy truth is that even well established artists usually teach or do something else outside their studios. Even among artists with international reputations, only a handful can afford to spend *all* their time in the studio. These are the few "greats" whose names are almost household words; leaders of some style momentarily in vogue, like the "abstract expressionists" who dominated the 1950s, or the "pop" and "op" artists who leapt to fame in the 1960s; a small circle of society portraitists; plus a few lucky mavericks who fit no current vogue, but whose style has somehow caught on. But most good painters, sculptors, and printmakers quietly accept fate and take some sort of outside job.

Why is it so hard for a fine artist to live on the sale of his work? Artists advance all sorts of reasons. Some say there can't be enough customers to buy all the art that's produced. The supply is said to exceed the demand. Others blame art dealers' business methods: high prices; inadequate publicity; too much emphasis on a small, upper class buying public; too little interest in selling art to the public at large. Still others point out that contemporary art is too complex to have widespread public appeal. And artists currently riding high emphasize that the art world is fickle: "Though you may be selling like mad, you can't be sure your luck will last. At any moment, the wind can shift. Then you're glad to have a steady job and a weekly paycheck."

Shelfloads of books have been written on the artist's problem. But this is no place to continue the debate. Whatever the reasons, you just can't count on being one of the lucky few who live on fine art. You *must* expect to earn your living some other way, perhaps teaching, perhaps in another art field, or even *outside* the art world. Fine artists accept this situation grudgingly.But they refuse to be discouraged. If this prospect *does* discourage you, fine art is no place for you.

Jobs for fine artists

Though fine art may be your first love, you must be realistic and plan ahead for the job that's going to earn you the income you can't get from your paintings, drawings, prints, or sculpture. There are plenty of jobs in other art fields, where you can make a decent living and still devote time to fine art.

Teaching seems to be the most common job among fine artists. Art schools, college and university art departments have expanded rapidly. Elementary, junior, and senior high schools employ more art teachers than ever before. Many museums now have art classes. There are art teachers in many YMCA's, YMHA's, and community centers.

Though teachers are poorly paid in comparison with other professions, many artists feel that teaching is the one job that allows enough time for studio work. You *don't* teach forty hours a week. You *may* not teach every day. And you get vacations that make non-teachers green with envy *if* you don't have to scrounge for a summer job to pick up extra money.

As I've said, many fine artists hold down 9-to-5 jobs in the applied arts. Others free lance from their own studios. Fine artists who work in the applied arts claim two advantages over teachers. If you're good, you can make more money. And many fine artists feel they'd rather spend 9-to-5 producing *some* sort of art, architecture, or design, even if it's not fine art. But holding down a 9-to-5 job or maintaining an active free lance practice, many artists complain that they spend all their creative energy. "When I get home at night," says one art director, "I've got nothing left for my painting. I just can't pick up a brush."

Short of inheriting a fortune, there's no ideal solution. There are pros and cons to *any* job a fine artist takes to earn his living. But you have to decide. You must pick a job that gives you reasonable satisfaction and a comfortable, if not luxurious, income. Having made your choice, you must then have the self-discipline to live a double life successfully. You're a teacher or an applied artist during "working hours," a fine artist whenever your time is free. You have to measure out your time and energy to handle both careers. You're like a runner who has two races to run in a single day: he must budget his strength to win both.

What does a fine artist study?

It's vital for a fine artist to pick his future job early, so he can plan a double education to fit his double life. In the right art school, college, or university, you can set up a program that will train you simultaneously for a career in fine art and a career in teaching or applied art. This is one more reason for choosing your school with care. Not all schools have a wide enough range of courses to perform this dual function.

If you're considering a career in fine art, you should still read the chapters that follow, each dealing with an applied art career that *might* be your job, even if your first love is painting, sculpture, or printmaking. Each chapter describes the job in some detail and tells you what applied art courses you should expect to take along with your fine art subjects. Certainly, if you expect to pair fine art with a teaching career, you should read Chapter 13 for a realistic view of the teaching profession and the training required.

Now, what fine art subjects can you expect to take? Though the professionals often disagree violently on what kind of training makes a good painter, sculptor, or printmaker, there *are* certain subjects you're likely to find in most fine art programs.

Painters, sculptors, and printmakers are all required to take lots of drawing. Classes normally draw the nude and clothed figure, plaster casts of sculpture, plus various other still life objects from bottles to bananas. When the weather is decent, you'll probably go outdoors to sketch the landscape, architecture, passers-by, and even the animals in the local zoo. You'll also be asked to draw from your imagination and try abstract experiments with line, tone, and texture. Instruction in the principles of perspective is standard. And you'll get a chance to try out a variety of drawing media: pencil, charcoal, pen-and-ink, brush-and-ink, wash (usually black or brown water-color), chalk, or even something exotic like silverpoint.

One brief word about drawing the nude. Life classes, as they're called in the trade, aren't an educational burlesque show invented by professional Peeping Toms. Artists' models are a tired looking, ill-paid, unglamorous crew. Life classes are bearable only because the nude figure teaches you more about the craft of drawing than you'll learn from still life, landscape or any other subject.

Few schools permit you to *major* in drawing, by the way, just as few professional artists devote their full time to drawing. In school, as in your professional life, you'll probably concentrate on painting, sculpture, or printmaking, with plenty of drawing courses thrown in. Of course, you may be one of those rare birds who wants to do nothing but draw. In that case, you may still be obligated to choose painting, sculpture, or printmaking as your *theoretical* area of concentration, but a sympathetic school should be willing to arrange your program to include more drawing than usual.

Painters are obviously expected to take a lot of painting courses, exploring such media as oil, watercolors, acrylic, tempera, casein, and pastel. Early classes usually emphasize still life. You then move on to landscape, the nude and clothed figure, portraiture, and abstract experiments. Painters rarely take sculpture classes, except during the foundation year, when most schools require some basic training in three dimensions. Printmaking, however, is often part of the painter's program.

But what *is* a print? Instead of painting a picture on a canvas or drawing it on a sheet of paper, the printmaker incises it on a copper plate, cuts it into a block of wood, or draws it on a slab of limestone with a grease pencil. The plate, block, or stone can be inked, covered with a sheet of paper, then run through a press. When the sheet of paper—the print—is peeled off, it carries the image that was on the copper, wood, or limestone. Thus, the print is an original work of art that comes from the artist's own hand. A great advantage of printmaking is that the artist can produce dozens of identical originals and sell them at a modest price.

The printmaking media are sometimes called the "graphic arts" or just plain "graphics." I've avoided these terms here to prevent confusion with the very different profession of graphic design, which will be discussed in a later chapter.

There are many ways to make prints, all more complicated than I've made them sound, of course, and the student printmaker tries various methods before he settles on one or more favorite techniques. You may try half a dozen ways of making prints from copper plates, like etching, aquatint, engraving and others. You'll probably try doing woodcuts and wood engravings. You may do lithographs on zinc plates as well as stone. Most often, you begin by working in black and white, then move into color printmaking when you've developed enough skill. You also have to accumulate *far* more purely technical information than the painter: about chemicals used to process plates and stones; about the mechanics of etching and lithographic presses; plus a thousand details about papers, inks, and other materials of the trade.

The painter-printmaker is a frequent combination. Just as painters generally take some printmaking classes, printmakers normally take painting. Sculpture also attracts some printmakers. Though few schools require printmakers to take sculpture beyond the foundation year, you should be able to elect advanced courses in this subject.

Though the painter and printmaker share many classes, the sculptor's training follows a very different road after the foundation year. You're most likely to begin by exploring a variety of materials and techniques. You may model clay figures; carve wood and stone; construct abstract forms in wood, plaster, metal, wire, paper. As you advance, you'll probably channel your energies into a specific medium: you may find you're most comfortable carving, rather than modeling; or you may discover that you do your best work in the new medium of welded metal. Naturally, your subject matter tends to be limited to the human figure, animals, and abstract shapes. Still life and landscape are more the territory of the painter and printmaker.

Sculpture, like printmaking, demands a lot of technical know-how. If you model in clay, you must learn to make plaster or metal casts of your clay originals. Building armatures—wood and metal skeletons inside clay figures—is a craft in itself. So is the manufacture of sculptor's tools. You may be expected to make your own chisels, hammers, and modeling implements. Of course, carving demands intimate knowledge of the quirks of each kind of wood or stone. And welded sculpture demands technical knowledge of metals. One well known sculptor says, "I'm not just a sculptor. I'm a carpenter, a plumber, and I could double as an auto worker if things ever got bad."

Few sculptors paint, and their training rarely includes much painting beyond the required courses. On the other hand, many sculptors are active printmakers in school and afterwards.

Art history forms an essential part of any artist's training. Knowing the work of the great artists of the past, you're better able to judge your own. You can also learn valuable lessons by studying their working methods. And one distinguished museum curator adds that studying art history is a kind of insurance: "Knowing what's been done before, you won't slave to come up with something that seems tremendously original, then discover it's old hat."

Instructors

There are often big philosophical differences between schools and even between instructors in a single school. One school may be dominated by abstract artists who just want to train other abstract artists. Another may be run by realistic landscape and figure painters who have no patience with abstract art.

Before you enroll, try to learn something about a school's bias, if there *is* a bias. Better still, try to pick a school where the instructors don't all work in the same style. It's healthy to have a wild-and-woolly member of the avant garde and a traditionalist teaching in adjacent classrooms. Each man has something all his own to offer you. When you've had a taste of both, you'll feel freer to develop a style of your own. Far from forcing you into a mold, a good art school, college or university art department hopes you'll profit by the differences among your teachers.

Does a fine artist need a degree?

No art dealer will ask if you have a degree before he exhibits your work. Nor will any purchaser. What matters is the quality of your work, not whether you can write B.A. or M.F.A. after your name.

However, if you plan to earn your living as a teacher, it's wise to pick a school that grants a degree. One noted painter comments bitterly: "If Rembrandt wanted to teach in one of our colleges, he wouldn't have much chance without a degree." A famous artist *can* sometimes land a top teaching position without a degree. But you can't be sure you're destined for fame. The chapter on teaching goes into degree requirements in greater detail. Here I'll simply point out that a bachelor's degree is a minimum requirement for most teaching jobs, and your bargaining power is even greater with a master's degree. If you're interested in public school teaching, you should pick an art school, college, or university with a special teacher training program that leads to a degree in art *education*.

How art galleries operate

The usual way for an artist to sell his work is through a gallery. Though most galleries pride themselves on looking non-commercial, the art dealer is essentially an agent who accepts goods on consignment. If he likes your work and thinks it will sell, he agrees to display what you produce. He pays the rent, but you owe each other nothing until he makes a sale. When he does sell something for you, he gets a percentage of the sale price. This can be as low as 25%, as high as 50%, but most often it's somewhere in between. The average is 33⅓%.

American galleries rarely *buy* the work of a living artist unless he's a really big name. Before he invests his money in a work of art, the dealer must be *sure* he can resell it at a profit. For this reason, most dealers play it safe. They pay you nothing and make no promises. All they ask is that you make no deals with competing galleries in the same city. They may have no objection to your having another dealer in a different city, too far away to compete. Nor can a dealer object when you switch to another gallery if he fails to sell your work. He may be just as pleased to sever the agreement.

Business arrangements between artists and galleries are usually informal. Written contracts are rare. It's a good idea to get a receipt for work you leave with a dealer. Artists and dealers sometimes agree to share expenses like framing, shipping, exhibition catalogs, and advertising. This agreement, with percentages specified, may be put into a short letter for the record. Of course, when a gallery is lucky enough to land a well known artist whose work really sells, the dealer may be willing to absorb all costs.

A gallery will exhibit your work in two ways: group shows with other artists handled by the gallery; ultimately a one man show devoted entirely to your work.

Though dealers' business methods differ in detail, this description fits most reputable galleries in the United States. However, rental galleries, sometimes called *vanity galleries*, are a different story. Though these galleries *look* like others, they're really nothing more than exhibition spaces for rent. You may hire the whole gallery or pay for each picture they hang in a group show. Any artist—good, bad, or indifferent— can arrange a one man show if he can pay the rental fee. If you can afford the additional expense, the vanity gallery may buy advertising space in newspapers and art magazines, make some attempt to get publicity, and arrange a cocktail party the day your show opens.

The big trouble with the vanity gallery is that you get so little for your money. As the words *vanity gallery* imply, you're buying nothing more than a boost for your ego. The gallery has no steady public. Collectors, critics, and museum people have all learned to stay away because they've seen so many second rate shows there. The only visitors likely to show up are your family, friends, and a few curious passers-by. Nor can you expect the owner to take any real interest in building your reputation for the future. His goals are strictly short range. He does no more than he's paid for, like a motel keeper renting you a room for the night.

Finding a dealer

Most art galleries are in larger cities, such as New York, Boston, Philadelphia, Chicago, Los Angeles, and San Francisco, and their suburbs. A few courageous dealers have opened galleries in out of the way spots like an island off the Maine coast or a California seaside town. But when these click, they usually owe their success to tourists and summer residents who come from big cultural centers—from cities.

This means you have to go to a sizable city to find a dealer, if you don't already live there. But don't just walk into the first gallery you see and try to strike a bargain. First you have to do some research.

Galleries tend to specialize. One may handle nothing but contemporary American artists, while another handles only French art. Some dealers show nothing but paintings, while others are known for prints and drawings. A gallery may become known for a particular style, like abstract expressionism, op art, pop art, or realistic painting with romantic overtones. Some dealers never show the work of beginners, but stick to artists with reputations. Others like to give young artists a start.

Before you begin your dealer hunt, you must get to know the galleries. Visit all you can and study each gallery's group of artists, sometimes referred to as the gallery's *stable*. A group show is a particularly good time to survey the entire stable at one crack.

You can also learn a lot about the galleries by reading exhibition reviews in magazines like *Arts* and *Art News*. Most big city newspapers have art critics who cover the local galleries. Since you can't possibly pay regular visits to the hundreds of galleries in New York, it's worthwhile to follow the *New York Times* art pages.

Having settled on a handful of galleries where your work might fit, you can start making contacts. Again, don't walk in without warning and expect the dealer to drop everything and spend an hour looking at your samples. Write or phone ahead for an appointment. If you can get an introduction from a teacher, collector, or established artist who knows the dealer, so much the better. Don't be surprised if the dealer asks you to send photos of your work before he agrees to see you. You might save him the trouble of asking: send some black and white photos or color slides with your first letter.

A dozen photos are enough to send, just to give the dealer a preliminary idea of your work. You'll probably want your photos back, so be sure to enclose a postpaid, self-addressed envelope. If you live far away and you're planning a special trip, be sure to say when you're coming to town.

Though not every dealer will read it, some recommend that you include a short biographical sheet with your letter. I don't think such a sheet means much if you're just out of school. If you're a beginner, it's probably simplest to include a few facts in your letter to the dealer: age, place of birth, academic honors, any well known teachers. If you're a seasoned artist, *then* you might put these facts on a separate sheet, along with a list of one man shows, with dates and places; juried shows (more about these in a moment) ; museums and well known private collectors who own your work. Try to hold yourself down to a page.

Don't expect everyone to write you an enthusiastic invitation. Some will turn you down flatly. Others will see you out of curiosity or because you've come through a mutual friend whose request they can't turn down. A few dealers may be genuinely interested.

When you do land an appointment with a dealer, he may ask you in on a special day he reserves for young hopefuls. Tuesdays, Wednesdays, and Thursdays are usually the quietest days in a gallery. One of these will probably be the day you're invited. Remember this if you're planning a trip from out of town.

When you select samples to show, remember these suggestions made by a New York dealer. Show examples of your dominant style. Though you may have been through several styles, just show the one style you want the dealer to remember. Equally important, show your dominant medium. Don't haul in work in every medium you've tried in art school. If your main interest is etching, just bring etchings. Don't confuse the dealer by bringing in a few wooden figures you carved one summer for a change of pace.

How many samples should you take to your first interview? If you're carrying prints or drawings, you can easily handle a dozen, unless they're unusually big. You'll probably have trouble carrying that many paintings, unless they're small watercolors. Half a dozen or even four will do. Sculpture is often impossible to carry around for interviews. Photos will have to suffice, plus a couple of small pieces *if* you do small things.

If the dealer is impressed, he'll come to the studio to see the things you couldn't carry. Or if you're too far away, he'll ask you to get hold of a truck and make that big second expedition. If the expedition is a success, you'll go home in an empty truck. Your work will go into the dealer's active stock.

The one man show

Though it's your dealer's responsibility to promote your work year after year, his most important single job is to give you a one man show. He'll hope to schedule such a show every two or three years, though this will depend on how much you produce. Some artists work so quickly that they have a show almost every year. Others work so slowly that five or six years elapse between shows.

What *is* a one man show? Your dealer turns over his whole gallery—or a large part—to you alone. Each piece in the show is numbered. The numbers reappear in a small catalog, with the name of the piece. Visitors can usually take catalogs free of charge. Prices are rarely listed, but anybody can find out prices by asking the dealer. When a piece is sold, a red star is pasted onto the frame or pedestal. A one man show usually runs three or four weeks.

Years ago, a one man show wasn't complete without a cocktail party on the opening day. This was fun for visitors, but rough on artists and dealers, who often shared expenses and were both broke after the party. In New York at least, the art public has finally recognized that most artists and dealers operate on a shoestring. Refreshments are no longer expected at most openings, though a few fashionable old galleries preserve the tradition. If an artist *insists* on drinks and food, no dealer objects as long as the *artist* pays the bill.

It's customary to take a small boxed ad in the art magazines and the art pages of local papers announcing your show. Artists and dealers may agree in advance to share this expense, plus framing and catalog printing costs. More often, the *artist* absorbs these expenses. If the artist has to invest a lot of money in frames, the dealer *may* share this too or perhaps advance some money against future sales. Instead of taking money from the artist, some dealers may accept a work of art.

Announcements, catalogs, and sometimes personal notes are mailed to the gallery's clients. A news release may be mailed to the press and a few photos of your work may be shot for local art critics, whom your dealer will try to bring in to review the exhibition.

Keep in mind that your dealer may not be able to give you a show immediately. Most galleries schedule exhibitions six months or a year ahead. The so-called *art season* runs from early fall through late spring. Don't be surprised if your show can't be scheduled till the following season.

Above all, don't feel that you must rush into a show as soon as you're out of school. An intelligent dealer may say, "Your stuff looks promising. Come back and see me in two or three years. Maybe *then* you'll be ready for a show." This is no brushoff. A one man show means you've achieved a certain maturity of style. Until you've reached this stage in your development, you can afford to wait. Many outstanding artists have worked quietly for a decade or more before they felt ready for their first show.

How important is a New York show?

Because New York is the nation's art capital, young artists often make great sacrifices to arrange an exhibition there. Many go into debt to pay their fare and freight costs for their work. And some go further into the red to hire a vanity gallery if they can't land a dealer.

Is a New York show worth all this? Does your future reputation really hinge on this one city?

Hundreds of one man shows open in New York every month. Critics race around town and review as many as they can, but bypass most for lack of time and newspaper space. Few shows sell enough to break even. Most get scant attention from the art public and are forgotten the day they close. Only a handful of shows cause any stir and most of these are forgotten too.

A New York show is worth striving for if you're realistic and recognize that you're betting on a long shot. Don't imagine that a New York show automatically means you've hit the top and all museums and collectors will open their doors to your work. A one man exhibition at a reputable New York gallery—not a vanity gallery—is worth a reasonable investment in time and money, on the *slim* chance that the art world's spotlight will swing your way for a moment. But it doesn't justify wiping out your bank account.

Across America, there are thousands of good artists who enjoy local reputations. Many of them have never had a New York show. They exhibit in local galleries and their work seems to sell as well—or as badly—as it might in New York. One museum curator explains: "A good artist will create his own audience sooner or later, wherever he lives."

Juried exhibitions

Another way of showing your work is in juried exhibitions sponsored by museums, local and national art organizations. The jury show is a free-for-all. Artists for miles around submit their work to a jury of well known artists, critics, museum men, or other authorities. The jury decides what to exhibit, what to reject. This same jury, or a separate group, may award cash prizes, medals, or certificates to entries judged outstanding.

Some jury shows are strictly regional: open to artists in a given city, county, state, or group of states. Others are national and a few are international. The artist usually absorbs the cost of packing, insurance, and shipping round trip. There may also be an entry fee, running as low as $2.00 or as high as $10.00.

The best way to keep track of forthcoming jury shows is to read the art magazines regularly and watch bulletin boards in museums and art schools.

There's great debate about the value of juried exhibitions. Those in favor feel that jury shows are a good testing ground for an aspiring artist. If his work is accepted, he can see how it stacks up when it's hung beside the work of his contemporaries. If he's turned down, he knows he has a way to go before becoming a real professional. Advocates of the jury system also point out that it weeds out second raters who don't really belong in the field anyhow.

Another theoretical advantage of the jury show is that it spreads the word about up-and-coming artists. Museum curators, collectors, and dealers *may* discover you. You *might* win a prize and get some publicity. And if you have no dealer, the jury show may be your only way to exhibit and perhaps make a sale.

However, there are also very damaging arguments against the jury system. Attackers say that no juror can avoid bias. A juror can't help favoring his friends and students—the art world is small—and liking styles similar to his own. Jurors *try* to be fair, but it's charged that personal differences in taste always lead to log rolling deals: "I'll vote for the picture you like if you'll vote for the one I like."

Not only are individual jurors said to be biased, but whole juries often lean toward a particular kind of art. Bring together three abstract painters and they may automatically turn down all traditional work. Conversely, a traditional jury may toss out anything abstract. Many annual jury shows pick the same kind of jury each year. The word soon gets around that only a certain style is likely to be accepted.

What this means, say attackers of the jury system, is that

such shows are *not* good testing grounds for young artists. A turndown doesn't necessarily mean you don't measure up. It may just mean you don't fit the jury's bias or you were squeezed out in a log rolling deal. Acceptance may be just as meaningless for exactly the same reasons. To make things *more* confusing, a picture is often rejected by one jury and accepted by another. It might even be argued that the best artists don't get into juried exhibitions because they don't conform to the tastes of any current clique.

Opponents of jury shows go on to point out that attendance is usually scant and sales are few. Although critics *may* write up big jury shows, only a few artists are ever singled out in the reviews. Few museum people see these shows, and many dealers frankly admit that they don't go and aren't impressed by an artist's long list of jury acceptances.

The final argument against jury shows is simply a matter of expense. You can spend an awful lot of time and money crating, insuring, and shipping things back and forth. For each piece accepted, some artists warn, you may have several turned down. It's common for a jury to receive 2000 submissions when there's gallery space for just 200. This means 1800 pictures *must* be turned down. This seems a very costly way to get your work shown. One artist observes wryly: "If you took the money you spent on jury shows and used it to rent an empty store for a month, you'd probably sell more stuff."

Whether submitting work to juried exhibitions is worthwhile, no one can say for certain. Though many good artists have given up sending things, the jury show remains an established exhibition method. If you do decide to invest in jury shows, be sure to investigate each jury and each show's history to see whether your work will fit in. Though you can never be *sure*, you can often predict which juries will be sympathetic to your style.

The role of museums

Besides backing juried exhibitions, museums often support

contemporary artists in two other ways. Many museums arrange shows of contemporary work *without* a jury. And many buy the work of living artists.

Like juried exhibitions, museum shows may be regional, national, or international. But artists don't necessarily submit their work to a jury for acceptance or rejection. Instead, the museum staff invites a limited number of artists to exhibit one or more things, which the staff may actually select from the artist's studio or gallery. Some museums actually try to sell things in the show. Others just refer customers to the artist or his dealer.

How do you get invited? Curators rely on their knowledge of the field, gained from visiting galleries, other museums, and juried exhibitions. If you have no dealer and don't participate in jury shows, you might send along a short note with some photos, requesting that the museum consider you. Some enlightened museums even have special days when they look at the work of newcomers.

Museums occasionally give some artist a one man show. This isn't for beginners. Nor can you *ask* to be given such a show. The museum reserves this honor for important artists with established reputations.

Museums purchase the work of living artists in very much the same way. They watch your development and buy something when they feel you're mature and important enough to be in the collection. They rarely take a flyer on an unknown artist. You can't just walk in and try to make a sale. The museum will come to *you* when they're ready. However, there's nothing wrong with you or your dealer sending over some photos and tactfully inviting a curator to visit your show or your studio.

No artist expects to live on sales to museums. There aren't enough museums and they often get a hefty discount from dealers. Artists and dealers are eager to sell to museums purely for the prestige. When an important museum makes a purchase, collectors often follow suit.

Portrait, mural, and monument commissions

Though most portraits are now done by photographers, there's still a certain amount of work for portrait painters and sculptors. If you have a dealer, he may find customers among his clients. A good dealer spends his leisure hours broadening his social contacts and may turn up portrait commissions in the process of circulating. Naturally, he collects his usual percentage of the sale price. Many leading portrait painters have no dealer, but ride the cocktail party circuit themselves.

Another source of portrait commissions is the satisfied customer. If a sitter is proud of the portrait you've done, he makes a point of showing it off to his friends. If a friend likes what he sees, he may be your next sitter.

Contacts are also the key to landing mural commissions, architectural sculpture, and civic monuments. *Social* contacts mean less than knowing local architects, interior designers, city planners, and members of the city fine arts commission, if such an agency exists.

There was a time when painters and sculptors were invited to submit models and sketches in competition for a big job. Though such competitions are still held here and there, most commissions are now awarded on the recommendation of the architect or designer doing the building. Art for public buildings and monuments may be commissioned directly from the artist by civic agencies. Again, one commission can lead to another. One successful mural or sculpture in a prominent location can set off a chain reaction.

Muralists and architectural sculptors must learn to be precise and hard headed about business dealings. Too often, a half completed project is suddenly canceled because of budget troubles, or a dissatisfied or indecisive client. To guard against losing his investment in time and money, the experienced muralist or sculptor often insists on being paid in three stages: one third of the price when the job is begun; one third when it's finished; one third when it's installed. He also expects to be paid for preliminary sketches or models, even if the job stops right there.

Other methods of selling fine art

There are many other places where you might exhibit and sell your work, particularly if you live where galleries are scarce.

Bookstores, furniture stores, and interior designers' shops often exhibit and sell paintings, drawings, prints, and small sculptures. There are even restaurants and coffee shops whose owners are delighted to liven up the walls with works of art *and* collect a percentage if a sale is made.

Some enterprising artists have saved their money and actually rented a store for a few weeks. In smaller cities, where everybody notices a new store and news spreads quickly, this has sometimes turned out to be a simple and profitable way of arranging a one man show. But even in a city as big as New York, I've seen this bold approach tried successfully.

A logical extension of this idea is the *cooperative gallery*. Instead of hunting for a dealer, a group of artists rent a store or a gallery where they can show their work throughout the year and share all expenses.

Not all successful artists exhibit their work publicly. I know a few who have sufficient reputation to sell directly from their studios. They rely on purchasers to send up *future* purchasers. The artist may have special visiting days or show his work by appointment, so people won't barge in and interrupt him at the easel. Though this system works best for well known artists, I'm told there are some little known men who sell this way and manage to build a small but faithful following. One popular idea is to buy a big, old house and convert a floor, a wing, or perhaps the barn into your own gallery.

The best known method of selling art without a gallery is the traditional sidewalk exhibition. How much work is *really* sold this way is anybody's guess. But I've met old timers who say it works.

Where can you get more information?

Though there's no nationwide art press in the United States, there are three monthly art magazines worth following. *Art News* and *Arts* are useful for critical articles on art history, current trends, and the work of major figures, past and present. *American Artist* is particularly valuable for articles that analyze the working methods of contemporary artists. Our one national newspaper, *The New York Times*, also attempts to cover art news across the country.

Another good way to keep up with the art world is to attend your local museum regularly. Most population centers now have art museums which show their own collections as well as traveling exhibitions and art films. Museums also have lectures, forums, and guided tours of the exhibitions. Many museums now have extensive art libraries.

To get the most out of your museum, it's worthwhile to pay $10.00 or $15.00 for an annual membership. For this small charge, you'll be kept informed about all museum events and you'll be invited to many that aren't open to the general public. You may get free admission to movies, lectures, and special exhibitions for which other visitors have to pay. You may get special publications—pamphlets, exhibition catalogs, books, even a museum magazine—prepared by the museum staff. The art library will be open to you. You may also get discounts on art books, reproductions, and magazines.

Finally, you should do your best to see all the important gallery shows and juried exhibitions that come your way.

6
Illustration

Of all the applied arts, the profession closest to fine art is illustration. You might say an illustration is simply a drawing or painting created for some practical purpose. Most often, the practical purpose of an illustration is to adorn or explain the printed word: a story, an article, an advertisement, or a book. Like the writer, the illustrator creates material for the printed page.

What does an illustrator do?

Illustration is a highly specialized profession. Your style, your interests, and "the breaks" will determine what field of illustration you choose.

Most familiar, I suppose, is the magazine illustrator. He creates the covers of our magazines, as well as the drawings and paintings that appear inside these covers. But there are even specialties within the magazine field. One artist's style lends itself to romantic stories in women's magazines. Another man's rugged style makes him a specialist in men's adventure magazines.

This is equally true in book illustration. One artist's style is just right for children's books. Another's style proves best for technical books and textbooks. And paperback covers are an important and specialized new field.

ILLUSTRATION 89

Advertising is a fertile field for the illustrator, but the enormous diversity of clients and products again encourages specialization.

Fashion advertisers—and the fashion magazines—have created their own special breed of illustrators. The fashion illustrator has a style quite unlike any other kind of illustrator. He devotes his life almost entirely to fashion ads and fashion magazines. He has just one subject: clothes.

Particularly in advertising—though also in magazine and book illustration—subject matter is often a specialty. Some illustrators are so good at rendering cars that they devote their lives to automotive advertising. An illustrator may become known for drawings or paintings of pretty girls, children, animals, food, or famous personalities. Soon he may find himself doing practically nothing else.

A medium may also turn into a specialty. Many illustrators work only in black and white. An artist may be best known for pencil sketches or pen-and-ink drawings. Someone else may make his reputation for a special way with watercolor.

Though cartooning seems a narrow specialty at first glance, even here you find a surprising number of fields. One cartoonist specializes in witty drawings for ads, stories, and articles with the light touch. Another's bold, masculine style leads him into adventure comic strips. A totally different craft, demanding special training or experience, is the animated cartoon for TV or the movies.

Where else might an illustrator's work appear? Pamphlets, posters, film strips, manufacturers' catalogs, scientific and technical publications, record album covers, greeting cards, political cartoons, packaging. These are just a few of the possibilities.

How much specialization is necessary? Must you be backed into a tight corner and stay there? This depends on your own abilities. If you're versatile enough, you can cut across several fields, like many magazine and book illustrators who also do advertising work.

But the fact is that every artist is strong in some areas, weak in others. Besides, advertisers and publishers need *so* many different kinds of artwork. No man can do them all. Even the most versatile illustrator soon develops a few areas of specialization. These turn out to be convenient and profitable because many clients remember you for your specialties.

There *are* situations, of course, in which an illustrator is hired for his versatility. If you work in a small organization, you may be expected to draw fashions one day and machinery the next. You may have to be equally skilled in color and black and white. You may do lettering, photo-retouching, and even photography in a pinch. But if you're like most aspiring illustrators, your goal is free lancing, which almost always means some degree of specialization.

Let me add an important footnote about the profession of illustration. When I was an art student two decades ago, illustration seemed the most glamorous of all the art fields. Illustrations dominated our national magazines; many illustrators were virtually household names and earned enormous incomes. Today, photographers get many of the assignments that used to go to illustrators. For example, fashions were once illustrated almost entirely by drawings; today's fashion magazines depend almost exclusively on photographs, while fashion drawings are used primarily in newspapers. Although there's still a reasonable amount of work for a good illustrator, it's no exaggeration to say that photography now dominates advertising and editorial art.

It's also fair to point out that the illustrator is at the mercy of rapid changes in taste. At one moment, the taste may be for realism; at the next moment, the trend may shift to a more decorative, linear, patterned style. In fact, this is just what's happened between the first and second editions of this book. Thus, the illustrator must not only face the powerful competition of the photographer, but must be resourceful and flexible enough to change with the times—or he's out of work.

Where does an illustrator find work?

As the last sentence implies, a large number of successful illustrators are self-employed. They earn their living by free lancing.

ILLUSTRATION   91

This means they have their own studios (or share space with some other artists) and take on assignments from many clients.

The main sources of free lance work are advertising agencies, magazine and book publishers, printers, public relations firms, plus the advertising, public relations, and sales promotion departments of stores and manufacturing companies. Some of these organizations have their own art departments, but even these departments often call for free lance help.

Don't take this to mean that an illustrator *must* free lance. Obviously, there are good 9-to-5 jobs—staff jobs, they're called —in the organizations I've just mentioned. The difference is that staff men are often used at the idea stage, not for the finished artwork. Most big advertising agencies, for instance, use their art departments primarily to hatch ideas and visualize them for the client in sketch form. When the client gives his go-ahead, a free lance is usually called in to do the finished artwork. Magazine and book publishers tend to work the same way.

Staffers *do* get to create finished artwork, but these are usually the smaller assignments. These might be black and white drawings for small ads and pamphlets, technical manuals, or posters used in the plant. Bigger, more ambitious illustrations tend to be given to free lance men, specialists in the subject or the style needed.

Because of this division of labor between staff and free lance artists, young illustrators are often advised to *start* in a staff job to learn the ropes. But the goal is free lancing.

However, not all staffers hope to free lance. Many illustrators take jobs in art services or art studios and stay there. An art service is a *firm* of artists—salaried employees, partners or even shareholders in a small corporation—who turn out artwork for a variety of clients. Many art services—art studio is just another term for the same thing—pay substantial earnings to top men who have no intention of free lancing.

In the field of fashion illustration, top people often hold down well paid 9-to-5 jobs with department stores or manufacturers. This becomes particularly vital when an artist's style becomes identified with a store's name or a manufacturer's product.

Many staff illustrators decide not to free lance because they *like* to concentrate on ideas and leave finished artwork to someone else. These men become art directors: planners and idea men with executive responsibilities in an agency, magazine, book publishing house, store, or manufacturing firm. At this point, the illustrator begins to fuse with the graphic designer—the organizer of the printed page—whose job I'll discuss in the next chapter.

What about geography? Most illustrators—staff or free lance—find work in big advertising and publishing centers like New York, Philadelphia, Chicago, and Los Angeles. However, the so-called communications business is becoming more and more decentralized. Every city big enough to have one or two daily papers and a TV station is likely to have an advertising agency. The nation's big industries, with their art and advertising departments, are scattered from coast to coast. In scores of cities, department stores hire staff artists and free lance artists too.

What does an illustrator study?

Above all, the illustrator is an acute observer of the life around him. Thus, the foundation of his training is drawing. He spends a great deal of time drawing the nude and clothed figure. Rapid sketches of the passing scene and precise renderings of still life objects are equally important.

Painting classes are also vital and these too emphasize observation. The illustrator paints a wide range of subjects: still life, landscape, abstractions perhaps, and especially the human face and figure. He explores many media: oil, watercolor, gouache, acrylic, pastel, any one of which he may use in his future profession.

Printmaking courses are often included for experience. Though books are sometimes illustrated with prints, the printmaking media are rarely used in advertising or publishing.

Note that all these fine art courses are *beyond* what the illustrator gets in his foundation year. Though every student gets a sampling of drawing, painting, and printmaking in his first

ILLUSTRATION   93

year, the illustrator is likely to take these subjects throughout his schooling.

There are also specialized courses in the illustrator's craft. These may be called "Illustration: Elementary, Intermediate, and Advanced." Or they may be divided into subjects like book, magazine, advertising, technical, and fashion illustration. In these classes, the student gets assignments that are meant to duplicate assignments he can expect on the job. Recently, a number of top schools have made photography classes available to illustration students.

Other specialized classes often include layout—the planning of the printed page—typography, and lettering. It's also essential for an illustrator to learn the mechanics of the printing industry: how type is set; how his drawings and paintings are made into plates for reproduction; how pages are printed.

Some schools offer a major in illustration: a program that prepares the student for any area of illustration he may decide to enter. Other schools may offer a major in some specialized field of illustration, like fashion drawing. This often includes courses in fashion design and the fashion industry. Many schools offer a broad major under the heading of *commercial art,* combining illustration and graphic design.

Does an illustrator need a degree?

All a client or a boss wants to see is your portfolio, not your diploma. If you have a degree, this *may* impress an employer who recognizes the value of a broad education. But few employers and *no client* will even ask.

What part-time and summer jobs are good experience?

While you're in school, the best summer or part-time job is obviously *anything* that gives you a peek into the workings of an ad agency, magazine or book publishing house, printing plant, or the art staff of a store or manufacturing firm. The job doesn't even have to be in the art department. You might learn valuable lessons in an agency's production department, where printing is ordered and followed through.

If you're especially good, you might even be able to pick up some free lance work from these sources while you're still in school. Even the smallest assignments make good portfolio pieces to prove you've had *some* experience when you go job hunting.

What is a typical first job?

In an advertising agency, art studio, or publishing house, you might be assigned to act as "Man Friday" to an art director or a more experienced illustrator. You'll probably run errands; paste type and photostats together for client presentations or the printer; mount drawings; fuss with files; and retouch photos. When you've won your boss' confidence, he'll ask you to sketch out some of his ideas, do some routine lettering, and draw small black and whites called *spots*.

In a store, these chores might be mixed with some display work and sign painting. A manufacturing company might add some technical illustration to the blend. A printing plant might also train you to handle production.

As you prove yourself, you'll get bigger and bigger drawings to do. You may move from black and white into color, from spots to more ambitious artwork. You'll begin to hatch your own ideas and do the finished art yourself or assign this to a free lance.

But if your goal is free lancing, why not just start free lancing as soon as you finish school? Top students often succeed in developing a salable style by the time they graduate. With a few summer or part-time jobs behind them, they may know enough of the ropes to start a modest free lance practice. They begin with small drawings and slowly work up to bigger assignments.

However, you have to be exceptionally good to start out on your own. Unless your teachers, friends in the field, and poten-

ILLUSTRATION   95

tial clients encourage you to free lance right away, it's best to begin by taking a 9-to-5 job. After a few years, when you've built up professional knowledge and contacts, you may feel ready to free lance. By then, of course, you may have risen so well in your job that you prefer to stay there.

What are later jobs like?

A successful free lance illustrator normally has his own studio, perhaps an assistant, and a variety of clients coming and going with all sorts of assignments. If he's lucky, he may have a few steady clients who virtually regard him as a member of their staff and feed him a stream of work throughout the year. The free lance may act as his own salesman, carrying his portfolio of samples from one prospective client to another. Or he may have an agent who carries the portfolio and collects a percentage of each check, often as much as 25%.

With deadlines every few days and a variety of clients to serve, the free lance illustrator is usually under pressure. Life is fast paced and hours are irregular. To enjoy this existence, you have to be tough, adventurous, well organized, and brimming with energy.

Though many free lance illustrators prefer to remain a one man operation, others build up a staff as business increases. This is how art services and art studios are born.

For the illustrator who prefers a somewhat steadier life— though *any* illustrator's life is fairly hectic—there are rewarding high level staff jobs. Magazine illustrators often become magazine art directors, who plan pictorial content and page layout. In the advertising business, a staff illustrator also tends to move up into art direction. A staffer in a store or manufacturing company may become head of the art department. All these men tend to move away from the drawing board as they take on executive responsibility. They hatch ideas and pass them on to other men—staffers or free lances—who execute the finished artwork.

The successful staff illustrator soon reaches a crossroads.

Either he becomes a planner, a decision maker, an organizer of other men's efforts, or he decides to stay with the drawing board and quits his job to free lance or join an art service that will pay him a top salary to produce finished artwork. At some point, the free lance may make the opposite move, of course. He may take a staff job as an art director.

Where can you get more information?

Illustration and graphic design are covered jointly in several good magazines and annuals. *Art Direction, Print,* and *CA: The Journal of Commercial Art* are magazines worth following. *American Artist* covers the work of leading illustrators as well as fine artists. *Graphis* and *Gebrauchsgraphik* are published abroad, but they are available here with English texts and they are widely read by American illustrators.

The *Art Directors Annual* and the new *Illustrators Annual* carry the work of top illustrators. The British *Penrose Annual* and the Swiss *Graphis Annual*, with English text, are also sold in the United States.

Many large cities now have local Art Directors Clubs, affiliated with the National Society of Art Directors. These local groups often hold exhibitions which you should attend. If you get to New York, or live there, you'll also find lively exhibitions at the Society of Illustrators.

And it hardy seems necessary to say that you should watch the books, magazines, newspapers, and other printed matter where the work of outstanding illustrators appears regularly. The periodicals room of your local library is a place you should get to know.

ILLUSTRATION   97

7

Graphic design

The graphic designer and the illustrator dominate the field sometimes called *commercial art*. Both men are concerned primarily with the printed page. While the illustrator creates paintings and drawings for reproduction, the graphic designer has been described as the *architect of the printed page*.

What does a graphic designer do?

The graphic designer creates a plan for the printed page—this plan is called a layout—then selects type, hand lettering, drawings, paintings, and photos. He may go even further and specify papers, inks, printing processes, and binding materials. His job is to organize all these elements into a harmonious and effective design.

This design may be an advertisement in a magazine or newspaper. It might be the magazine itself, a pamphlet or a book, planned page by page on the graphic designer's drawing board. The design may not always be a printed page. It might also be a poster, a record jacket, a television commercial, a film strip, a package or even a display unit in a store.

A graphic designer is sometimes a specialist, sometimes not. There *are* free lance graphic designers who'll design anything a client may ask for, from a trademark the size of your fingernail to a trade exhibit 100 feet square. On the other hand, many graphic designers do specialize. Advertising and magazine art directors rarely design books, while book designers rarely do anything else. Some graphic designers concentrate on television. Package design has become an important specialty. Many graphic designers specialize in exhibits and mass produced display units, which brings them closer to industrial design, the subject of a later chapter.

A graphic designer may become so fascinated with typography that he becomes known as a designer of type faces or a hand lettering expert.

The designer may or may not create the finished artwork for his layout. In a large organization, he's likely to call on other staffers or free lances for illustrations, photographs, and lettering. In a small organization, operating on a low budget, the graphic designer may act as his own illustrator and lettering man, at least some of the time. A handful of unusually versatile men manage to divide their time between layout and illustration, but the tendency is to specialize in one field or the other.

Where does a graphic designer find work?

Probably the best known graphic designer is the art director who works for a magazine or an advertising agency. Art studios and art services also employ graphic designers, as do the advertising and art departments of stores and manufacturing companies. Book publishers and printers often have a graphic design department, while typographers sometimes hire a graphic designer who has a special interest in type. Display houses hire graphic designers who want to specialize in three dimensional advertising. Industrial design offices use graphic designers for packaging jobs.

These are all 9-to-5 staff jobs, but every one of these organizations also uses free lance talent. Even an art studio with a large, versatile staff may use a free lance when no member of the firm has exactly the right style or experience.

In illustration, the juiciest assignments go to the free lance, but this isn't true in graphic design. A graphic designer may do very ambitious work on a 9-to-5 job. It's hard to name a famous illustrator who isn't a free lance, but I can name scores of leading graphic designers who have 9-to-5 staff jobs. The choice between staff work and free lancing is a matter of temperament. Opportunities are equally good on both sides of the fence.

Should you start free lancing right after school? Some illustrators try this successfully as I've said, but few graphic designers can manage it. Graphic design is more technical than illustration. There's much more to absorb about the mechanics of printing, advertising, and publishing. It's far easier to learn the tricks of the trade in a staff job than on your own. A beginning free lance can feel terribly lost without a good nuts-and-bolts staff job behind him. It usually makes sense to start out in a staff job and *then* try free lancing when you know your way around.

The geography of the graphic design profession is something like illustration. The big advertising and publishing centers— the big cities like New York, Detroit, Chicago, Los Angeles —are the main job markets. But there are now many good jobs in ad agencies, studios, stores, and manufacturing companies in smaller cities. The book and magazine publishing business is still centered in New York, Philadelphia, and Chicago, but many smaller publishing organizations are springing up in unexpected places and creating job opportunities. Many universities, for example, have set up publishing operations in out-of-the-way spots. The traditional pilgrimage to Madison Avenue no longer seems so necessary.

What does a graphic designer study?

The graphic design student may find his subject called many different things, depending on his school. Instead of graphic design, it may be called advertising design, commercial art, advertising and editorial art, or even something as baffling as commercial design.

Beyond the basic fine art and elementary design classes of the foundation year, you can expect various classes in layout, with practical assignments in the design of ads, mailing pieces, pamphlets, magazine pages, posters, and packages. There may be special classes dealing with production: the mechanics of typesetting, engraving, printing, and binding. Typography and lettering are common subjects. Some schools have special courses in package design, television design, and display work.

Most graphic design programs include a fair amount of illustration. The mixture may be half-and-half if graphic design and illustration are given under the heading of commercial art.

Photography now appears in many graphic design programs, as schools build studios and darkrooms. A handful of schools are lucky enough to have facilities for typesetting and printing, so students can actually turn out small pieces of printed matter. One well known school *requires* each graphic design major to design and print a small book.

Does a graphic designer need a degree?

In graphic design, as in illustration, a degree means less than your portfolio. Since graphic design requires a good deal of technical know-how, *some* employers may take your degree as evidence that you've had the necessary courses. But a degree is hardly a requirement of the profession, as it's become in fields like industrial design and architecture.

What part-time and summer jobs are good experience?

You can learn *something* valuable from any low level job you might be able to land in an advertising agency, publishing firm, printing house or the art department of a store or manufacturer. Even if your job has nothing to do with art—you're more likely to be a glorified office boy—you can learn a lot just by being around artists, copywriters, and production people.

Jobs in such places may not be so easy to get, particularly if your home or school is in an out-of-the-way place. What other summer or part-time jobs might contribute to your professional background? I'd recommend *anything* related to the printing business, even if it's an errand boy's job in a small town printing shop or a stock boy's job in a paper house or a bindery. Or I'd try for any job that allows you to use a pencil or a brush. Even as a sign painter or a sign painter's helper, for instance, you may learn important secrets about lettering.

If you hope to be an advertising agency art director, you might find that a selling job in a store teaches you a lot about the consumer for whom your ads will someday be designed.

What is a typical first job?

An advertising agency often assigns a beginner to assist a seasoned art director. The beginner gets his on-the-job training by looking over the art director's shoulder and doing his routine chores. The newcomer runs his boss' errands; mounts layouts and artwork; pastes type, photostats, and artwork together for the printer; retouches photos; may do some small drawings; and eventually does small layouts under the boss' supervision. When the beginner has proven himself, he's allowed to develop small layouts on his own, then more ambitious ones as he gains experience.

A magazine's art department may follow a similar procedure or you may be given some specialized job to do. You might be assigned to assist a photo editor for a while. Or you might work on just one section of the magazine, which you and your boss lay out each week or each month.

In a printing house, you'll also start out assisting someone and eventually get a chance to do small layouts, lettering jobs, and perhaps minor illustrations for small clients who don't have their own art department or can't afford a free lance.

The pattern is more or less the same in a book publishing house, store, manufacturing firm or art studio. You start out as someone's "Man Friday," then slowly win greater freedom as you prove yourself.

What are later jobs like?

A senior art director in an agency may be assigned to one or more clients. He may design all of the client's advertising, from newspaper ads to TV commercials. Or he may share the account with other art directors in the office, each of whom handles a different phase of the advertising campaign. He works closely with the clients, as well as with the agency's own copywriters and researchers. He often has a beginner assisting him. And he constantly interviews free lance designers, illustrators, photographers, and lettering men.

The agency art director is expected to know more than graphic design. He is an expert on selling products.

A magazine art director is also more than an artist. He is a journalist. He knows how to pick the right picture or series of pictures to tell a dramatic story. He knows how to lay out a page that will intensify that story by the intelligent use of type, color, and other design elements. The art director may design his publication from cover to cover—except for the ads, which agency people design—or he may divide various articles and sections with other art directors. Like the advertising art director, he interviews free lance talent. He also works closely with the editors and writers whose pages he must plan, and he sometimes goes on location with to direct photographers .

The book designer in a publishing house not only designs the book page by page, but is often deeply involved in book manufacturing. Design and production are often handled in the same department or in overlapping departments. The situation is similar in many printing plants, where the designer may be concerned with production.

The graphic designer in an art service functions very much as he would in an agency. Agencies themselves may be among his clients. So may the other organizations I've just mentioned. For illustrations and finished art, he may turn to other staff members or call in a free lance.

The free lance graphic designer may get assignments from any of the staff men I've listed. Sometimes he carries his own portfolio and acts as his own salesman. Or he engages an agent to drum up clients and collect a percentage of sales. He may be just a one man organization and prefer it that way. Or he may find himself building up a staff, really his own art service, if business really booms. He probably has a few steady clients, plus many others that give him scattered jobs. The free lance designer may call in other free lances—illustrators, photographers, lettering men—and deal directly with typesetters, engravers, printers, and binders. In short, he may supervise the whole job for his client. Or he may just be paid to create layouts which his clients put into production.

Whether he works 9-to-5 or maintains the erratic hours of a free lance—some designers manage *both*—the graphic designer usually works under the same pressure as the illustrator. In the field of advertising and editorial art, there are always publication deadlines to meet, unpredictable clients to satisfy, and jobs to be done at desperate speed.

Where can you get more information?

Graphic designers read the same magazines as illustrators, plus a few others. *Art Direction, CA: The Journal of Commercial Art,* and *Print* are the three leading American magazines in the field. *Package Design* is a magazine recently begun for designers interested in packaging. The British monthly, *Design,* straddles several design fields, but often has worthwhile articles on advertising and editorial art. *Graphis* and *Gebrauchsgraphik,* both European publications, have English texts.

The *Art Directors Annual* is the leading American publication of its kind. The British *Penrose Annual* is available in the United States. So is the *Graphis Annual.*

Like the illustrator, you should certainly see the annual exhibitions of the local Art Directors Clubs in various major cities. The traveling exhibitions of the American Institute of Graphic Arts are always worth seeing if they come your way. And you should train yourself to examine every handsome piece of printed matter you come across.

8
Fabric design

Fabric design, like illustration and graphic design, is too often regarded as an extension of painting. This is partly true of *printed* fabrics. But most fabric designs are *woven* and the construction of a woven fabric is really a form of three dimensional design.

What does a fabric designer do?

The name *fabric design* hardly describes this complex profession, which embraces many specialties and reaches into several big industries.

The fabric designer who springs to mind first is the man who creates the printed patterns that appear on dress fabrics, blouses, scarves, upholstery, curtains, and dozens of other things we wear or buy for our homes.

But the *weaver* is also a fabric designer. The designer of printed fabrics creates a pattern to be stamped onto the surface of a piece of cloth. The weaver, on the other hand, literally constructs the cloth, interlocking fibers to form a built-in design. He may really be a hand weaver, actually turning out fabrics on his own loom. More likely, he's a designer of woven fabrics turned out by machine for a mass market. One man *may* master both techniques, printed *and* woven fabrics, but most designers specialize in one or the other.

However, fabric designers don't necessarily design fabrics. A designer of printed fabrics may also create wallpapers or even *specialize* in this field. The decorative patterns on linoleum, wall and floor tiles may be developed by fabric designers. So may decorative plastics for upholstery, wall covering, table tops, and other interior items.

Fabric designers may also design rugs, knitted and embroidered fabrics, shower curtains, lampshades, towels, linens for the bedroom and dining room, wrapping paper, decorative screens and wall hangings, wallboard, and *any* surface that might be enriched by design.

Though the designer may concentrate on one field or cut across *several* during his professional life, he must get to know whatever industry he enters. If he designs dress fabrics, it's helpful to have a thorough knowledge of the fashion industry. If he designs upholstery fabrics, floor and wall coverings, it's extremely useful to know the home furnishings industry.

Where does a fabric designer find work?

The greatest number of fabric designers have 9-to-5 staff jobs. They're employed by manufacturers of printed and woven fabrics, wallpaper, linoleum, carpeting, and all the other products I've mentioned. A handful work in design studios similar to art studios in the commercial art field. But there are very few of these and only a limited number of jobs.

The would-be free lance designer—one man selling work to a string of clients—floods the fabric design field and has a terribly tough time surviving. Here and there, weavers have set up their own shops, producing cloth by hand and selling directly to the public. Like free lancing, this handcraft approach seems like a difficult way to earn a living. Occasionally it works.

But the best opportunities are staff jobs with manufacturers, most of them in the eastern half of the country. The nerve center of the textile industry is New York, where most design studios are located and where many manufacturers and converters have their design departments. There are also many jobs in the plants themselves, scattered along the east coast from New England to the southern states. Manufacturers of other products, like plastics and floor tile, may be scattered as far as the midwest.

A surprising number of fabric designers divide their time between New York, the capital of the fashion and home furnishing industries, and the far-flung towns where plants are located.

What does a fabric designer study?

Courses in two and three dimensional design are basic. Painting and printmaking also appear on many programs. The purpose of all these is to develop your fundamental design sense. Though these subjects appear in the foundation year, they're often carried right through your senior year.

Practical courses normally include assignments in many fields: fabrics for fashion and home furnishings; wallpapers; accessories like scarves and place mats; decorative patterns for linoleum, plastics, and other synthetic materials. You're taught how to print fabrics with silk screens, stencils, wood and linoleum blocks.

Weaving may be required, available as an elective, or even a major in itself. Most art schools, college and university art departments emphasize hand weaving. This has brought criticism from professional designers and manufacturers, who point out that hand weaving bears little resemblance to the enormously complex operations of a textile mill. They charge that hand weaving classes are not adequate training for a future designer of mass produced woven fabrics, who must really combine the skills of the artist with the technical knowledge of a textile engineer. One well known designer says: "If I could re-live my school days, I'd spend four years in a good art school and then switch to a textile engineering school."

A few schools have profited by these criticisms and begun to broaden the technical training of fabric design majors. Because fabric design is so strongly linked to fashions and home furnishings, many schools offer special courses introducing you to these industries. In general, a greater effort is being made to make the training of fabric designers more professional.

In some schools, fabric design may be called textile design or pattern design. The subject may also be offered as part of a general major in fashion, since the largest number of fabric designers go into the clothing industry.

Does a fabric designer need a degree?

A degree is not a requirement, but if you do have a degree from a school that offers extensive *technical* training, an employer is likely to be impressed. As in other design fields, the number of fabric designers with degrees is on the rise.

What part-time and summer jobs are good experience?

The logical summer or part-time job would be something in a manufacturer's design department, no matter how low level your duties. You might find such a job in the textile industry or in some other industry that uses fabric designers. There's also a slight chance that you might find a job in a design studio, perhaps as a replacement for a junior designer who's on vacation.

There are many jobs outside industry that might be good experience. Selling fabrics, wallpapers, linoleum, and similar products in a department store will teach you a lot. In fact, any store job in fashions or decorating will add to your background. You might also look for a job in the fashion industry itself.

What is a typical first job?

As in most art fields, a beginner usually starts out assisting an experienced designer. You'll make color sketches of senior designers' ideas and perhaps try color variations of your own. You may weave samples of new design ideas if weaving is your specialty. For presentation to management or clients, you may create precise renderings of your bosses' design ideas in paint or in woven samples.

Later, when you've won your employers' confidence and absorbed the necessary technical knowledge, you may be turned loose to work out your own designs. But this day may be far off if you hope to design woven fabrics and you lack the technical background. One noted designer-manufacturer says frankly, "I have to start most beginners from scratch, just as if they never went to school."

Though this description fits most beginners in the textile industry or a wallpaper manufacturing firm, a newcomer's life in most other industries follows the same lines. In any industry, there's a lot of technical detail to absorb before you really begin designing. In the plastics or linoleum industry, for example, the designer must be educated in the properties and manufacturing problems of a material that may be totally unfamiliar.

What are later jobs like?

The senior designer in a manufacturing firm is responsible for creating his own design ideas and following them through from sketches to the stage when they're ready to be produced. This means that he does more than sit at a drawing table. He works closely with the engineers—textile engineers, chemists, plastics experts—who supervise production. He may work with the researchers who study what the public will buy and with the marketing men who sell his designs. With these men, he plans new product lines. He may design these products himself or, if he's the top man with the title, "design director," he may sketch out his ideas and pass these on to his staff.

In the textile industry itself, senior design jobs may be broken down into specialties. A colorist, as his title implies, concentrates just on colors: predicting and promoting color trends, determining the most salable color combinations, and coordinating the colors of product lines. A stylist, on the other hand, may do no actual designing. His job is to organize product lines, selecting and orchestrating various products much as a graphic designer organizes the elements on a printed page.

A few designers have succeeded in establishing studios, with a staff serving a variety of clients. The number of these studios remains small, but it seems to be increasing. A fair number of designers have expanded into manufacturing, producing the fabrics they design.

Since most successful fabric designers hold staff jobs, they aren't subjected to the same kind of pressure as men in free lance fields, like illustration. There aren't quite as many rush jobs or dry spells when you wonder where your next assignment will come from. But the fashion and home furnishings industries are among the most unpredictable in our fast paced economy. The textile industry itself has had violent ups and downs in recent years. Keeping up with the rapid shifts of public taste and trends in the industry itself—in fashions, these shifts take place several times each year—takes a quick mind and involves as much pressure as any job I know. Many fabric designers say that theirs is the most volatile of all the art professions.

Where can you get more information?

The leading magazine is *American Fabrics*, rather expensive for a student, but usually available in a good library.

Aside from this, there are no magazines published just for fabric designers, but you can learn a lot from publications in related fields. The fashion magazines, with their rich pictorial content, are a splendid source of information. Among these are *Vogue, Harper's Bazaar, Mademoiselle, Glamour,* and *Seventeen.* The daily newspaper of the fashion industry is *Women's Wear Daily.* The home furnishings press also devotes a lot of space to fabrics, as well as to wallpapers and floor coverings. *Interiors* and *Interior Design* are the leading magazines. *Home Furnishings Daily* is the newspaper.

It also pays to dip into magazines like *Architectural Record, Progressive Architecture, Architectural Forum,* and *Industrial*

Design for information about new flooring materials, decorative plastics, tiles, and other products developed by fabric designers working *outside* the textile industry.

Craft Horizons usually has important articles about hand-weaving. So does *Handweaver and Craftsman*.

Though there's plenty to read, the most valuable information is always gathered first hand. You have to haunt the stores where fine fabrics, wallpapers, fashions, and furniture are sold. You have to attend fashion shows and go to see new public buildings where fabrics, floor and wall coverings are intelligently used. Wherever you go, you must be a constant observer. Everyone's clothes, everyone's home may contribute something to your education if you're always on the alert for a fresh idea.

9

Interior design

The term *interior designer* may be new to you. The interior designer used to be called an *interior decorator*. But the profession is rapidly abandoning the word decorator. As you'll soon see, decoration is just one of the designer's responsibilities. He does far more.

What does an interior designer do?

The interior designer selects and organizes the furnishings of homes and offices, as well as hotels, banks, restaurants, and other public places. He determines what furnishings are needed, then decides where these will be located. He determines a color scheme and chooses furniture, fabrics, carpeting, wallpaper, lighting fixtures, and other items to fit into his plan. He prepares plans like those drawn by an architect, makes sketches in color, and may even build scale models of fully furnished interiors to explain his ideas to the client.

This is more than a *decorative* arrangement. The interior designer must often work within functional limitations, like walls he can't move and built-in lighting. The designer studies the tastes and living habits of his clients. The interior reflects their personalities and meets important functional requirements. The arrangement of furnishings is convenient. The furniture itself is comfortable and durable. The room is easy to clean and *keep* clean. The lighting and color scheme relax the eyes. Like the architect, the interior designer plans the environment in which people must live and work. In Scandinavia, he's called an *interior architect*.

Beyond the job of *designing* or *redesigning* an interior, there are all sorts of practical problems which the interior designer must consider. If there's any construction to be done, any furniture or fixtures to be built in, he must supervise the work. He must be on hand to make sure that furnishings are properly placed, that paint matches his color scheme, and that wallpaper goes on the right walls. This means dealing with contractors and overseeing the work of carpenters, electricians, painters, paper hangers, and other craftsmen. Naturally the designer is expected to prepare cost estimates for his clients and make sure these estimates turn out to be accurate.

The interior designer is often brought in to work with the architect when a new building is in the formative stage. Many enlightened architects and their clients now insist on this, so that interiors will harmonize with the total concept of the building and not look like an afterthought.

Beyond residential and commercial interiors, the interior designer may plan the passenger accommodations of ships, trains, buses, and airplanes; room settings for motion pictures, television shows, and stage plays; model rooms to display products on sale in stores; experimental interiors for magazines; window displays, exhibitions, and trade fairs.

In fact, the interior designer may work on more than interiors. He often develops custom made furniture for his clients. Many designers create lines of mass produced furniture, manufactured for sale in department stores and furniture stores. Others are drawn into some specialty like the design of lighting fixtures, which brings them close to the field of industrial design, the subject of a later chapter.

The designer may also specialize in some important area like supermarketing planning, hotel work, offices or residential interiors. Some interior design firms have built national reputations on such specialties. However, many designers move freely from one specialty to another or work in all these areas at once.

Where does an interior designer find work?

Many interior designers are really in the furniture business. They're employed in furniture stores or in the home furnishings sections of department stores. Others have their own shops, selling furniture, fabrics, lamps, and various accessories. These men will plan an interior without charge on the condition that the client buys his furnishings from the designer. The designer's income is his profit on the sale of the furniture.

Interior designers may also work in design offices or may open design offices of their own. These design consultants have no stock of furniture, fabrics or any other products to sell. They're more like an architectural office or an art studio: a group of designers selling a service. Many operate simply on a fee basis or on a percentage of the total cost of the interior. Other design offices, particularly small ones, may make their money as stores do, by selling furnishings. Still others combine these methods of payment: they collect fees for their services *and* commissions on sales.

Interior designers are also drawn into manufacturing. Some design for furniture manufacturers, on a full-time or free lance basis. Makers of automobiles, airplanes, buses, and trains hire interior designers for full-time staff jobs or free lance work. A handful of designers manufacture their own furniture.

There are often jobs for interior designers in other kinds of design offices. Many architectural offices and industrial design firms now have interiors departments.

Other employers include hotel chains, which are constantly putting up new hotels and refurbishing old ones; store planning departments of supermarket chains; builders and contractors who find it useful to offer interior design services as an inducement to clients; even women's magazines, which hire designers to create interiors for how-to-do-it articles.

Interior designers are scattered across every state in the country. There are jobs and free lance work for interior designers in every population center big enough to have department stores, growing suburbs, and an expanding business district. This description fits *hundreds* of cities, large and small, where there are homes, offices, stores, and public buildings to design, furnish, and redesign. Interior design, unlike fabric design, is a highly decentralized profession.

What does an interior designer study?

After the introductory fine art and design courses of the foundation year, you soon find yourself planning actual rooms. This means more than selecting and arranging furnishings. You make sketches of interiors in pencil, watercolor, pastels, and other media. You build small, precise models of rooms, including tiny reproductions of furniture, lamps, drapes, rugs, and wall coverings. You draft plans and elevations of interiors, similar to architects' blueprints.

There are often separate courses in model building, drafting, sketching, and rendering. These are all methods you'll use to explain your ideas to clients and contractors when you're on the job.

You may also take courses in color; the fundamentals of architectural construction; window and store display; graphic design for signs and displays in public places. Another *must* is usually a class in the history of art and architecture, with special emphasis on the great interior styles of the past.

Furniture design may be a special course or even a major subject within the interior design curriculum. Again, this means building models, not just tiny scale models, but full size furniture. A course in furniture design almost always means a good deal of time in the woodworking shop. You'll not only learn the principles of good furniture design, but manufacturing methods and the structural properties of materials like wood, metals, and plastics.

Beyond the required program, you may be able to choose several elective courses like fabric design, ceramics, and even industrial design, to which furniture design is closely related.

The American Institute of Interior Designers, by the way, lists the following subjects as a "Proposed Degree Course in Interior Design": interior design; graphics and color; structural design; history and theory of art, architecture and interiors; furniture design and construction; mechanical equipment of buildings; experimental design; working drawings and specifications; and professional practice. Also listed are such liberal arts subjects as English, a foreign language, contemporary civilization, sociology, history of science, psychology, and literature.

Does an interior designer need a degree?

Though many good interior designers never got a degree, it *is* significant that the most influential professional association in the field recommends a degree course. I doubt that many AID members would consider a degree indispensable when they hire a new staff member, but the AID's stand indicates that a degree has strong selling power.

What part-time and summer jobs are good experience?

Though it may be hard to find, the best summer or part-time job is an apprentice spot in a design office, designer's shop, or the interior design staff of a department store or furniture store.

A selling job may also be excellent experience and might be easier to get. You can learn a lot about home furnishings by selling furniture, fabrics, rugs, lamps and lighting fixtures, wallpaper, and similar products in a department store or furniture shop.

Skilled trades like carpentry or upholstering can teach you a lot. It's worthwhile to try for a part-time or summer job in a cabinet maker's or upholsterer's shop.

Another excellent spot might be a drafting job in an architectural, engineering, construction or manufacturing firm *if* your drafting is sufficiently advanced. Speaking of manufacturing, you might also try for a job in a plant that makes home furnishings. Even a production line job in a furniture factory would be valuable experience for a future furniture designer.

What is a typical first job?

Like most apprenticeships in the art field, your first job in interior design will probably be a motley assortment of low-level chores that teach you more than you realize. For instance, you may take care of filing furniture catalogs and photos, and samples of fabric, wallpaper, wood, and paint. This will teach you the materials of the trade, as well as *sources*, the hundreds of places where you can find the furnishings and accessories that fill an interior.

Beginners are often used as shoppers, another good way to learn about products and their sources. On instructions from senior designers in your office, you visit showrooms to select samples and photos of furnishings that might be suitable for a current design project. You check prices, delivery schedules, and the merits of competing products, slowly building your own mental file of essential data.

At first, you may not get a chance to design any interiors on your own, but you'll sketch, draft, render, and perhaps build models of other designers' ideas. You may compile presentation folders of fabric, wallpaper, paint, and wood finish samples for clients. You may also assemble books of photos or sketches for client presentations.

In a store or shop, you may sell and advise customers on their choice of furnishings. This experience will give you insight into public taste and buying habits. It will also develop the poise and verbal skill needed to deal with clients.

What are later jobs like?

As you prove your ability, you're given projects of your own. You develop interiors with less and less supervision. You draft and sketch *your own* ideas. You begin to deal directly with clients, examining their needs and making recommendations. And you supervise the work of contractors who build, supply, and install the furnishings you order.

Climbing toward the top of the ladder, you must ultimately

face the choice of continuing to work for someone else or having your own business. You may become a key man in a design office, or head of the interior design department in a store or architectural office. You may decide to open your own shop or design office. If you end up in manufacturing, you may become design director of a furniture company, for example, or you may even decide to design and manufacture your own furniture.

In a top job in a larger organization—whether you're self-employed or on someone's payroll—your time at the drawing board will be limited. Your main functions will be to deal with clients and management—if you're in manufacturing—and make decisions. You may develop design solutions in broad terms, then hand the details over to staff members down the line. If you're in manufacturing, you'll also spend a lot of time thinking about marketing problems and planning new product lines.

Your own small design office or shop may also limit your time at the drawing board, if only because you have to be a Jack-of-all-trades. You and one or two assistants may do everything: dealing with clients, designing, shopping, supervising contractors, and keeping up the files. As one designer put it: "In the morning I roll up my sleeves and work at my board. At lunchtime, I put on my jacket and spruce up for lunch with a client. For the rest of the afternoon, I'm not a designer, but a businessman calling on prospects. Then I rush back to the office before dinner to write a few letters, clean up the office, and empty the waste baskets."

Your relationship with your clients depends on the nature of your business. If you concentrate on residential interiors, steady clients are rare. Since it's obvious that few home owners redecorate year after year, most of your work boils down to one-shot jobs, though many clients may buy new items of furniture from time to time. Designing commercial interiors may mean lots of one-shot clients who want a store or office done. But chains of stores, hotels, banks, and other firms with many branch offices may provide a steady stream of assignments over the years. The same may be true of shipbuilders and manufacturers of automobiles and airplanes, who constantly develop new products that need interiors.

Where can you get more information?

The leading magazines for interior designers are *Interiors* and *Interior Design*. The trade newspaper is *Home Furnishings Daily*. There are also mass magazines, influential and richly illustrated, like *House Beautiful, House and Garden,* and *Better Homes and Gardens*. Nearly all the women's magazines and the women's pages of the daily newspapers devote extensive space to interior design.

The architectural magazines carry lots of material valuable to interior designers. The three leading architectural monthlies are *Architectural Forum, Architectural Record* and *Progressive Architecture*. The British *Architectural Review* is available in the United States.

Other design publications, not specifically in the field of interiors, are widely read by interior designers. Among these are the American *Industrial Design*, the British *Design*, and the Italian *Domus*, which blends architecture and interiors and carries an English language supplement.

Certainly the best way to learn more about the field of interior design is just to keep your eyes open. Visit new— and old— public buildings that have notable interiors. Browse in furniture stores and in the home furnishings sections of department stores. Above all, develop the habit of looking carefully at every room you enter. In the years to come, you may design and redesign many such rooms.

10
Architecture

More than any other artist, the architect is responsible for planning the surroundings in which we live. The interior designer may create our rooms and the furnishings that fill them, but the architect shapes the buildings that contain these rooms. He shapes the landscape that surrounds these buildings. He may even plan parts of the *entire* city.

What does an architect do?

The architect designs buildings and supervises their construction. This simple statement gives no hint of the complexity of the architect's job, perhaps the most complicated of all the art professions.

Before he touches pencil to paper, the architect must study the living habits of the people who expect to live or work in his building. It's no exaggeration to say that a good architect is a skilled psychologist and social scientist. He must examine the zoning laws and other regulations of any locality where he plans to build. This means he must be a legal and real estate expert. He must analyze the client's finances to determine cost limitations. Obviously, the architect needs a good head for figures.

When he finally draws plans for the building, he must come up with more than a handsome exterior. The building's location on its site must reflect the architect's knowledge of traffic conditions, weather, and the terrain. In a large building, there must be adequate corridors, stairways, elevators, entrances, and exits for normal traffic and for any emergency. The plan for the building itself must make proper provisions for plumbing, wiring, heating, and air conditioning. Above all, the architect's plan must make logical use of space and not waste an inch. One critic has said, "Architecture is the art of space."

But the architect's plan must do even more. Beyond the job of organizing the areas of a building, the architect is responsible for the *structure*. His elaborate detail drawings must show how the building is put together. Pages and pages of diagrams explain details like window construction; the design of stairways; the anatomy of walls, floors, and ceilings. These drawings must indicate the location of such mechanical elements as heating and air conditioning units; elevator and escalator machinery; lighting equipment and plumbing. Naturally, each sheet carries exact dimensions of every stick and stone.

From this mass of detail must emerge an object of beauty, showing the sculptor's sense of form and the painter's ability to handle color, texture, light and shade. A building must be both "a machine for living" and a work of art.

However, the architect's job still isn't done when his design is completed. He must then select all the materials that go into his building, from bricks to light switches. This demands an encyclopedic knowledge of the thousands of materials and devices currently on the market.

The architect is expected to work closely with several consulting engineers—structural, mechanical, heating, and electrical experts—when the building is complex enough to require such a team. When the structure is ready to go up, the architect deals with the contractors and watches them like a hawk to be sure they follow his plans and specifications accurately. There may be *scores* of contractors—the builders, plumbing, heating, and electrical contractors are just a few—who need constant supervision until the building is completed.

Though many architectural offices will design *any* kind of building, from a tiny beach house to a multi-story office building, others specialize. Some architects concentrate on houses.

Others are best known for schools, hospitals, or other public buildings. Office buildings have become a specialty because of their enormous complexity. Stores and shopping centers have recently emerged as a lucrative specialty. The list goes on indefinitely.

An important and neglected specialty is landscape architecture. Using trees, shrubs, grass, stones, bodies of water, and the shape of the terrain itself as his building materials, the landscape architect literally reconstructs our natural surroundings. Architects who design buildings often design their own landscaping. But landscaping is really a specialty, and the landscape architect is called in as a consultant to work closely with architects and city planners.

City planning is another specialty that attracts many architects. As his title suggests, the planner designs cities or parts of them. The design elements he works with are *groups* of buildings, blocks, streets, bridges, tunnels, parks, public transportation systems, the terrain, and thousands of minor objects like street lights and parking meters. He redesigns today's cities and plans future cities. He's not only a skilled architect, but an expert on population trends, traffic, water supply, mass transportation, local politics, and a huge list of other factors that influence the day-to-day life of every city.

As if they don't have *enough* to do just practicing architecture, many architects also design furniture, lighting equipment, and other accessories for their buildings.

Where does an architect find work?

Most architects are hired by architectural firms. These are essentially consulting organizations. That is, they accept work from a variety of clients: corporations putting up new buildings; real estate men and builders planning housing developments; families who want to build new homes.

Some architects get staff jobs in industry. Corporations with long range building programs—supermarket chains, hotels, manufacturers with far-flung plants and office buildings—often have an architectural department. There are also jobs with builders and real estate firms. Other kinds of consulting firms—engineers, industrial and interior designers, for example—frequently have architects on the staff. Federal, state, and local governments employ a number of architects full-time, usually on the basis of civil service examinations.

Geographically, architecture is quite decentralized. There's work for architects wherever people are putting up new buildings or revamping old ones. Logically, most architects are located in or near metropolitan areas, simply because that's where they find the most people and the greatest building activity. But there are successful architects in every city of reasonable size, as well as in many small towns.

What does an architect study?

Because an architect's work involves public health and safety, all states require a license for the practice of architecture. Though licensing requirements vary from one state to another, a standard requirement is usually graduation from a recognized professional school, usually a five year program, plus three years of experience in an office headed by a licensed architect.

Are all licensed architects graduates of five year programs? Most states are intelligent enough to recognize that years of experience, usually ten or twelve, are equivalent to a five year diploma. However, architectural school graduates have two advantages. As I've mentioned, they can get a license sooner. Furthermore, architectural school programs are carefully planned to cover the territory of the licensing exam. Though it seems unfair to penalize the man who couldn't afford five years of school, this exam can be rough going for the architect who lacks formal training.

Are *all* practicing architects licensed? Actually, there *are* men who work for years without a license and who may never get one at all. However, they must work *under* a licensed architect who must take legal responsibility for the drawings. An unlicensed architect can get a job, but he can't rise very high or start his own firm.

Your first year in architectural school may be planned as a foundation year, but it won't be the same as an art school's foundation year. There are usually basic courses in two and three dimensional design, freehand drawing and drafting, perspective, plus an introduction to architectural design and construction. Mathematics, with strong emphasis on geometry, is likely to be important. And since the five year program leads to a degree, you'll begin your long series of academic courses in the liberal arts and sciences.

In succeeding years, you'll plunge more deeply into the principles of design and construction. You'll design small structures, then bigger ones, from the sketch stage to detailed working drawings that contractors could actually work from. You'll cover acres of paper with your drafting. You'll build models and learn to render buildings in pencil, pen, and watercolor for presentation to clients. You'll learn a special lettering style for putting data on drawings.

There will be courses in landscaping, city planning, and the history of art and architecture. There will be technical subjects like mechanics, strength of materials, physics, equipment for buildings, construction costs, specification writing, real estate, and professional practice, which means the way an architectural office functions. There may also be classes in areas of special interest like housing, office buildings, reinforced concrete and other materials.

Landscape architecture and city planning, I might add, may be given as separate majors or areas of concentration within the general architectural program. City planning, in particular, is often given as an advanced degree program *after* you've gotten your bachelor's degree in architecture.

If this heavy program of architectural subjects leaves you any free time, you may get a chance to take a few classes in painting or sculpture, perhaps the greatest lack in the programs of our architectural schools.

You'll find, by the way, that many architectural schools require two to four years of college *before* you're admitted.

Does an architect need a degree?

Though it's possible, as I've said, to get a job and even a license without graduating from an architectural school, there's no question that a degree from a recognized school is a great advantage in job hunting. It's possible to take some short courses in drafting and elementary architecture, start at the bottom in an architectural office, and work your way up. But advancement is easier and faster for the man who has the complete training symbolized by the degree.

What part-time and summer jobs are good experience?

A good student in a respected school can often get a summer or part-time job in an architectural office. More quickly than other art professions, architects have recognized the value of such jobs, particularly summer jobs, as ways to test young people whom they might want to hire after graduation.

If you can't get a summer or part-time job in an architectural office—which usually means routine drafting—*any* drafting job will be useful experience. Local construction firms, manufacturers, or engineering firms may have a temporary spot for you as a draftsman.

It's also worthwhile to investigate fields *related* to architecture. What about a job with an electrical, plumbing, or heating contractor; a supplier of building materials; a real estate firm? Any organization linked to the construction business provides an opportunity to build up experience while you're still in school.

What is a typical first job?

A beginning job usually means drafting. The junior draftsman starts out reproducing other men's drawings with a few revisions. When you prove your skill and judgment on such lower-level assignments, you'll be given rougher drawings, sketches, or just ideas to interpret in finished line drawings. You're not really designing yet; but architecture is a complicated business, demanding great precision, and it takes real ability even to interpret another man's concepts on paper.

In a big office, you're likely to find yourself assigned to one department, doing a rather specialized job for quite some time. The design department, where the big ideas are hatched, may seem far away, perhaps in some remote part of the office. If you're being groomed to be a designer, it may still be a while before you actually move to the designers' department. On the other hand, if your bosses feel that your future lies in some other area—construction supervision, for example, or specification writing—you may be headed for some other part of the office. Only a small percentage of architects actually do design work in a big organization.

A small office is more likely to make you a Jack-of-all-trades from the very beginning. In addition to routine drafting, you may do some renderings, build some models, and even get a chance to watch construction and deal with contractors. Does this mean a smaller office is a better place for a beginner? It's true that a smaller architectural firm may give you more diversified experience. On the other hand, you may never work on the big projects that land in bigger offices. There's also the factor of temperament. Some beginners enjoy the often hectic pace of a small office, where everybody does everything. Others like the feeling of bigness and the knowledge that you have just one job to do well. Experienced architects often recommend that you start in a small office and then move to a big one to see how the other half lives.

What are later jobs like?

After several years, if you're good, you move into the category of senior draftsman. In a large architectural office, this means you can be charged with quite an elaborate set of drawings, which you can produce with a minimum of supervision.

As you climb the ladder in a big office, you'll almost certainly move into a specialty. Young architects tend to feel that design is the most glamorous specialty. On the contrary, many find rewarding spots as job captains, in charge of teams of draftsmen producing the great sets of working drawings from which structures are built. Others enjoy supervising construction. Analytical minds may lend themselves to specification writing, which means an analysis of the items and materials that go into a building's construction.

The odds in favor of your doing *some* real design, after three or four years, seem to be better in a small office. This doesn't mean you'll design a building from top to bottom, but you may get a chance to contribute ideas and solve certain design problems. Having started as a Jack-of-all-trades, you can expect more of the same as you climb the ladder. Design, drawings, specifications, construction supervision, and client contact all become interwoven. There may be *some* specialization at the top—one partner may be particularly good at working with clients, while another is best at supervision—but you must all be prepared to handle *any* aspect of a job.

When you've risen to a key position in an architectural office, large or small, you may become an associate, roughly equivalent to a junior partner in a law firm. Later you may become a full partner. Partners and associates get a share of the profits in addition to their salaries. And they obviously have some say in how the business is run.

For most architects, the long range goal is to set up one's own practice. If you become an associate or a partner in an existing firm, of course, then you *have* your own business without going out and opening your own office. But you may not wait that long. You may be a one man office, hiring junior draftsmen when you have a big push. Or you may share responsibilities with a partner or two, adding temporary or permanent staff as business expands. Ultimately, you hope, you'll have a full scale organization of your own.

Though architecture is the oldest and best organized of the art professions, it's no more stable than any other free lance business. The ebb and flow of clients remains a problem. Men are hired for a project and must be released when the building is finished, unless there's a new client to keep them busy for a while longer. The dividing line between permanent and temporary jobs is indistinct. Job hunters get used to being told, "The job's permanent as long as the work holds out." This is particularly true in New York.

Where can you get more information?

The leading American architectural magazines are *Progressive Architecture, Architectural Forum,* and *Architectural Record. House and Home* specializes in the home building industry. The British *Architectural Review* is certainly the best magazine published abroad. The Italian *Domus* is widely read here and has an English language supplement.

Architects also follow the rest of the design press. *Interiors* and *Interior Design* are important reading for architects. *Industrial Design* covers a field that now attracts many young architects. The British *Design* is also available here.

Architectural exhibitions are few and far between, but there are important ones circulated from time to time by New York's Museum of Modern Art and the American Federation of Arts. Watch the calendar of your local museum for such shows. The local chapters of the American Institute of Architects also hold exhibitions which you should attend.

The way to learn most about the profession of architecture is to look at buildings. Try to get around and see the best buildings, large and small, in your area. Go inside if they're open to the public. Visit parts of your town that are being "redeveloped" by the city planning commission. Architecture is all around you, waiting to be looked at.

11
Industrial design

Comparable to architecture in complexity and breadth of training is the new profession of industrial design. Since the first appearance, in the late 1920s, of men who called themselves industrial designers, the field has grown so rapidly and in so many directions that no one has come up with an adequate definition for the profession. One spokesman says simply: "The industrial designer is a kind of modern Leonardo da Vinci. He must be prepared to design anything from a spoon to a city."

What does an industrial designer do?

To the public, the industrial designer is best known as a designer of so-called hard goods: cars, refrigerators, TV sets, stoves, air conditioners, and scores of other household devices from can openers to electric mixers.

But this is only one of the spheres in which industrial designers operate. They create many other household objects: furniture, lighting fixtures, tableware, the toys in the nursery, the tools in your tool box, the plumbing fixtures in your kitchen and bathroom, even your door knobs.

Industrial designers work on industrial products as well: products manufactured for use by industry itself. Among these are machine tools, trucks, farm machinery, electronic instruments, and office equipment such as typewriters and adding machines.

The armed forces now use industrial designers to work on weapons, tanks and troop carriers, aircraft, and atomic submarines. The transportation industries—builders of planes, trains, buses, and ships—use industrial designers to plan passenger accommodations. Industrial designers have been drawn into architecture and interiors, particularly stores, banks, service stations, and other commercial buildings. A related field is exhibition design and display work. Though packaging might be called a form of graphic design, since packages come off the printing press, many industrial designers are active in this field.

Because the industrial designer does such diverse things, few laymen can figure out just what the designer does to all these products. The designer is often described as a sort of stylist: "He puts all that fancy stuff on cars." Certainly, the designer's most obvious job is to make a product good looking, though I might add that most designers shudder when people connect them with jazzy cars. Nevertheless, the designer's job is to boost sales, and *one* way is to design a handsome product.

But most good industrial designers also say their job is to make a *better* product. Just as the architect must design a building in which life runs smoothly, the industrial designer must create a product that is safe, comfortable, and convenient to use. This is why the armed forces hire industrial design consultants: military men don't much care how a tank turret looks, but they want to be sure the gunner is comfortably seated, his weapons are convenient to handle, and he doesn't whack his head when he swings around. Industrial designers apply this same sort of thinking to non-military products. The designer is an expert on the way people and products work together.

He must also have a basic knowledge of engineering, since he works closely with engineers in developing a product and planning its manufacture. It's the engineer who creates the mechanical part of the product, while the designer works on the parts we see and touch. Thus, the industrial designer needn't be a trained engineer, but he must know enough about fundamental principles to talk the technical man's language.

One leading designer has summed up his profession in words that may seem discouraging to some readers, inspiring to others:

"The industrial designer is an almost impossible combination. He should blend certain qualities of the painter, sculptor, architect, engineer, graphic designer, medical man, and super salesman. No man can be all these things, really, but the industrial designer has to try."

The industrial designer combines all these skills because he's responsible for the *working relationship* between man and the manufactured objects we live with. This responsibility demands that the industrial designer, like the architect, be *more* than an artist.

Depending on his background and his job, the industrial designer may do highly diversified work or may choose a specialty. In some consulting design offices, you might get a chance to work in all the fields I've mentioned. But you might also specialize in some particular family of products, like appliances, cars, or packaging. A material may become a specialty: some designers work just for the aluminum or plastics industry. A handful of men design no products at all, but become experts on lighting or color.

Where does an industrial designer find work?

The nation's industrial designers are divided between consulting offices and the design staffs of manufacturing corporations. The design consulting firm, like an architectural office, has a variety of clients, usually in non-competing fields. For this reason, a consulting office usually has many kinds of products on its drawing boards. A job on the design staff of a manufacturing company normally means that you work on a more limited range of products. If you work for a manufacturer of electric ranges, for instance, you'll obviously concentrate on ranges, perhaps with some packaging and display work thrown in. Some manufacturers *do* make a diversified product line, which may mean more diversified work for the design staff.

Even with a full design staff, a manufacturing corporation may still retain a consulting design office. Just as a designer might find a 9-to-5 job in any of the industries I've mentioned, the consulting office finds its clients in these same industries. Many designers move back and forth from jobs in industry to jobs in consulting firms.

Most consulting offices are located in large cities centered in the nation's industrial regions. New York and Chicago are the nerve centers of the consulting business, though there are successful industrial design firms in a score of other cities. Philadelphia, Los Angeles, Milwaukee, Akron, and Pittsburgh are just a few examples. Wherever manufacturers are clustered, there are opportunities for industrial design consultants.

Staff jobs are scattered completely across the map, wherever a manufacturing plant might be located. A factory can be in a major city, a small town, or a rural area. Though consulting is a fairly centralized business, a corporate staff job might take you anywhere in the United States.

What does an industrial designer study?

Following the foundation year courses which you share with other art students, you'll move into more advanced courses in two and three dimensional design. Quite soon, you'll be introduced to basic engineering, materials, and manufacturing methods. You'll learn drafting and model making. You'll explore various sketching and rendering techniques.

But learning these techniques will mean far less than learning to solve *practical design problems*. Most important of all, you'll take courses in which you design actual products, just as you would in a design office. At first, you'll probably start with small products like hand tools or kitchen utensils. By your final year, you may have tried anything from major appliances to railroad cars. You may find your design courses divided into categories like product design, which usually means hard goods; transportation design; exhibits and displays; packaging, and so on. Or these subjects may be mingled in a series of classes labeled industrial design: elementary, intermediate, and advanced.

Supplementing these professional courses may be related subjects like graphic design, architecture, interior design, and even photography, a valuable tool in design research. None of these will be advanced courses, but they're useful additions to your background. You can also expect introductory classes in business methods. And if there's any time left, you may be encouraged to take a bit more painting, perhaps some sculpture or ceramics to strengthen your sense of three dimensional form.

Some schools have begun to emphasize courses, or at least assignments, in research and report writing. Psychology and the social sciences are often stressed. Marketing is becoming a subject of major importance. Courses in *human engineering* are on the rise. This rather pretentious phrase means the study of the human body: how it's constructed, how it operates, and how we can use this information in designing better products for human use.

Does an industrial designer need a degree?

Though there's a movement afoot to introduce licensing, the practice of industrial design doesn't require a license. Thus, the degree isn't essential, as it is in architecture. There are many first rate designers without degrees, particularly among older men who entered the field before schools had industrial design programs. But among younger designers, a degree is an important qualification in most employers' eyes. This is particularly true in manufacturing companies. The best industrial design schools, like architectural schools, offer degrees. A degree has come to stand for the most complete professional education.

What part-time and summer jobs are good experience?

The first place to look for a summer or part-time job is a consulting design office or the design department of a manufacturing company.

Part-time jobs are usually hard to find in such places, but summer jobs seem to be increasing. Like architects, many industrial designers use summer jobs to test and train future employees. A few design offices have found a way of combining summer *and* part-time work: the student is tried out for a summer, then kept on for one day each week during the school year if he makes the grade. Many good design schools are willing to plan your schedule so you can work in a design office one day and attend classes four days.

However, if such a job can't be found, there are other fields where you can pile up some good experience. Any kind of drafting job—in an engineering or construction firm, for example—is valuable background. Many manufacturing corporations need draftsmen too. You can also learn a great deal from a job in which you work with your hands or with machinery: a carpenter's shop or a machine shop can be a good place to learn about how things are put together and how they work.

Since the industrial designer is supposed to be the closest thing to the *universal designer*—the man who can do anything—almost *any* art job might be valuable experience. Look back at the chapters that precede this one. Any part-time or summer job I've suggested for a graphic designer, interior designer, or architect might be a good suggestion for an industrial designer.

Perhaps the easiest summer or part-time job to get is a selling job in a store. This may seem far from industrial design, but an understanding of consumer psychology, what sells and why, is essential for a designer. Such a job can be extremely valuable.

What is a typical first job?

A beginner's main job, as in most other art professions, is to put his bosses' ideas on paper. You spend a lot of time drafting other men's designs. Your ability to sketch and render will also be put to work. A design often goes through hundreds of sketches—just for study purposes, not for the client—before it reaches final form. If your renderings are really first rate, you may be asked to create finished presentation drawings for the client.

In the same way, you may build models based on the drawings and suggestions of more experienced men. These models may be clay, plaster, wood, metal, plastic, cardboard, even paper. Some will be just study models, sketches in three dimensions. Others will be presentation models, built to explain an idea to the client convincingly.

If you join a large design office or corporate design staff, you may find that the work is departmentalized. You may be assigned to the product design group, packaging, interiors and display, the model shop, or some other subdivision. A small consulting office or corporate staff is less likely to be specialized in its organization: here the Jack-of-all-trades is wanted. A few manufacturers employ hundreds of designers, divided among many departments. At the opposite extreme, some consulting design offices contain just a boss and an assistant.

What are later jobs like?

As you advance in the industrial design profession, you may become a senior designer or perhaps a department head in a consulting office or corporate design staff. Ultimately, you may become design director of a corporation. You may become an associate—a sort of junior partner—or even a partner in a consulting design office. You may finally decide to launch your own consulting organization.

In a manufacturing company or a large design office, the senior designer concentrates on contact work and developing ideas. His job is to create design concepts and supervise junior designers who put these concepts in the form of drawings and models. He does a good deal of sketching himself, plus a certain amount of drafting, while he is exploring design ideas. But he leaves model making, rendering, and more routine drafting to younger men.

If he works in a consulting office, he must work closely with his clients' engineers and marketing men to make sure the design is practical and salable. Keeping the client sold is a major job in itself. If the designer is on a corporate staff, of course, these engineers and marketing men are his colleagues.

But he must work closely with them and *sell* his ideas just as if they were clients. So then, the senior designer is an idea man, an administrator, and a contact man.

However, if you start your own one or two man consulting firm, then you may have to be junior designer and senior designer all at once. You're your own draftsman, model maker, renderer, researcher, client contact man, and above all, the salesman who wins future clients.

Where can you get more information?

There's only one American magazine devoted specifically to the industrial design field. As you might expect, it's called *Industrial Design*. However, most alert designers also read the British *Design* and many follow the Italian *Stile Industria*, which carries an English language supplement.

Since the industrial designer's interests embrace the entire world of design, the magazine rack of a design office often includes the leading architectural magazines, *Architectural Forum*, *Architectural Record*, and *Progressive Architecture*, plus the British *Architectural Review;* the top home furnishings magazines, *Interiors* and *Interior Design;* graphic design magazines like *Art Direction, Print,* the *CA: Journal of Commercial Art,* and the Swiss *Graphis,* which includes English text; *Package Design;* and *Craft Horizons.*

Exhibitions of industrial design are rare in the United States, but most designers would say that the real exhibition center for design, both good and bad, is your local department store. A tour of any large department store will tell you more about contemporary design (good and bad) than you can learn any other way.

12
Photography

Photography is an art so new that artists still argue about whether photographs are really art. This debate will probably go on for years. But for the purpose of this book, I think we can accept the photographer's conviction that a camera, like a brush or pencil, is just one more tool for creating pictures.

What does a photographer do?

Though photography is barely a century old, the camera already performs an amazing variety of services and the field has become quite specialized.

The portrait photographer is probably most familiar. According to one professional association, this specialty attracts a greater number of budding camera men than any other kind of photography.

The phrase, commercial photography, like the equally vague phrase, commercial art, covers a number of specialties. These include many kinds of advertising photography, from fashions to food, any one of which can be a specialty in itself. Publicity pictures—anything from theatrical personalities to a new office building—also come under this heading. The magazine photographer may be asked to illustrate articles on a *variety* of subjects. A so-called commercial photographer may work in *all* these fields at once. But there's an increasing tendency to specialize in one or a few of these areas.

Particularly in advertising, publicity, and magazine work, subject matter is likely to become a specialty. Many photographers are known entirely for their fashion pictures. Architectural and interior photography is an important specialty. Some men are best known for travel pictures, theatrical portraits, automobiles, food, or industrial subjects.

Photo-journalism has become a field in itself. The best-known photo-journalist is the newspaper photographer, who covers the news with a camera as the reporter does with his notebook. The picture magazines, like *Life* and *Look*, have developed their own kind of photo-journalist, who specializes in *picture stories*.

Industrial photography is another vague term that covers many different activities. The industrial photographer may call himself that because he does advertising and editorial pictures for business magazines. Or he may actually work in the plant, photographing stages in the development or manufacture of a new product; recording the results of tests made by the research department; shooting pictures for advertising, publicity, or company magazines; making film strips to train new employees; illustrating catalogs of the company's products.

Scientific photography may range from photomicrography, which means shooting through a microscope, to astronomical pictures.

Motion picture and television photography are complex fields that are often subdivided into specialties. Some motion picture men are known for Hollywood extravaganzas. Others concentrate on intimate, informal documentary work, the motion picture equivalent of photo-journalism.

I might go on for several more pages, naming other specialties within the expanding world of photography. Some men work almost entirely in color. Some specialize in film strips and other visual aids. There are legal photographers who use the camera to assemble evidence for the courtroom. There are medical photographers, police photographers, baby photographers, and even livestock photographers!

Where does a photographer find work?

Like illustrators and graphic designers, photographers can choose between free lance work and a staff job. Many regard free lancing as their goal, even if they start in a staff job. However, there are also staff jobs that offer a good future to the photographer who prefers a less hectic life.

Magazines—which means not only consumer magazines like *Life* and *Look*, but trade publications and company magazines —may have staff photographers or use free lance talent. Many publications rely on both. Book publishers rarely hire staff photographers, but often use free lances. Newspapers and news services, on the other hand, rely mainly on staffers, but there may be opportunities for free lances too, particularly in the pages of Sunday magazine sections of big city papers.

Advertising agencies and public relations firms are unlikely to hire staff photographers, but use free lance talent on a large scale. Department stores sometimes have staff photographers, but more often use free lances, especially for large advertising campaigns. Manufacturing companies often have large photographic staffs and even small companies may have one or two photographers. In addition to staffers, many manufacturers use free lances.

Motion pictures are essentially a free lance business. The camera man is usually hired by the producer to shoot a particular movie, TV commercial, or perhaps a series of short films. A few motion picture companies have staff camera men, who may be supplemented by free lances when a big production comes along. Motion picture news services—they make newsreels for TV and movie theaters—usually hire staffers. So do TV studios, which must have camera men working around the clock.

When a free lance finds his business expanding rapidly, he may begin to take on a staff, unless he prefers to remain a one man business. When a photographer takes on a staff, his organization is called a studio, and there are opportunities in such organizations for 9-to-5 jobs. The studio may even hire free lance talent when there's an overflow of work. Many large commercial studios have a handful of free lances on call.

Other clients for the free lance are practically unlimited. Just about everyone has a portrait photo made at some time. Nearly every business needs advertising and publicity photos of new products, personalities, facilities. Most public institutions must document their activities: museums, for instance, normally use a staff or free lance photographer to record every object added to the collection. It's no exaggeration to say that nearly every individual, corporation, and institution employs a photographer for *some* reason, sooner or later.

Though many photographers prefer to work alone, I might add that nearly every successful photographer may be a potential employer. Sooner or later, there's a chance that he'll need an assistant.

What does a photographer study?

There's not much agreement among photographers about the ideal training for a career in photography. What confuses the issue is that a number of talented men have become successful photographers *without* any real training. Among the most famous photographers is a former button salesman who just taught himself to take pictures in his spare time. There are just enough self-taught geniuses like him to perpetuate the legend that photographers need no training, just experience. Unhappily, for every successful, self-taught photographer, there are dozens who try to teach themselves and fail.

Most photographers agree that professional training is needed, but many question whether training in *photography* is vital. They point out that many of our best photographers attribute their success to fine art training. Some of these top professionals took a few photography courses. Others took none at all. But they all had substantial training in drawing, painting, and design.

Another faction admits that while many of our best photographers started out as fine artists, illustrators, and designers, these men were trained *before* most schools had photography programs. There was no choice but to take *other* art subjects and do spare-time work in photography. Now that it's possible to take extensive courses in photography—this faction argues—training in other art subjects seems less vital.

What this means is that the experts seem to approve two kinds of training for professional photographers. One kind emphasizes fine art and design courses *as well as* photography courses. The other program sticks to photography.

Let's look first at the fine-art-plus-photography program. Here you'll probably start with the same foundation year as other art students: basic courses in drawing, painting, and design. *After* the foundation year, you're introduced to photography. First, you work in black and white with one simple camera. You learn to process your film and make prints in the darkroom. You learn basic principles of optics and photographic chemistry. Later, you're introduced to other cameras, large and small; color photography; motion pictures; and specialized subjects like fashion, photo-journalism, portraiture, architecture, and product photography. You spend lots of time learning the subtleties of lighting and how to direct models. Throughout these years, you continue to draw, paint, make prints, perhaps sculpt, and you'll certainly take advanced classes in experimental design.

In the program that concentrates entirely on photography, you'll probably plunge directly into camera work, without any introductory art courses. At the outset, you're likely to get a lot of technical training in photographic chemistry, optics, sensitometry, mathematics, and a subject sometimes broadly titled photographic science. At the same time, you get your first camera assignments. You learn to process film and make prints. You're introduced to lighting, composition, black and white and color photography.

You then move into advanced subjects like advertising, fashion, architectural, and portrait photography. There are often specialized courses in photo-journalism and photo-illustration. You'll spend many hours on experimental darkroom techniques. You'll explore the special technical problems of motion pictures. All in all, your training will be far more technical than it would be in the program that blends fine art and photography.

Which program makes a better photographer? Advocates of straight photography programs—no fine art—say their students have much greater technical skill and spend more class hours actually taking pictures. Those who argue for a blend of photography and fine art say their students think more creatively. Both arguments are convincing: leading photographers have been trained by both methods.

The American Society of Magazine Photographers (see Chapter 20 for their address) publishes a list of college level courses in photography.

Does a photographer need a degree?

Though a degree always adds a bit to your ammunition when you go job hunting, it's a rare employer who *asks* if you hold a degree. No client will care.

What part-time and summer jobs are good experience?

You'll learn something from any job in a photographic studio or the photography department of a publisher or manufacturer. You might be nothing more than an office boy—still good experience—or you might land a spot as a junior darkroom technician, helping to process film and make prints.

If you're really skilled with a camera, even though you're still a student, you might be lucky enough to get a part-time or summer job actually taking pictures. Local portrait studios sometimes use part-time photographers, particularly for assignments like weddings and mass orders of portraits for school yearbooks. Summer camps and resorts sometimes hire photographers for a few months at the height of the vacation season. And you certainly might try to get free lance assignments from friends who want portraits, or even from local businesses.

Even if you can't get a job in photography, there are many worthwhile summer and part-time jobs in related fields. Any job in the communications business—advertising, publishing, publicity—will teach you something about a field where photography is used. If you're taking the kind of photography courses that include art training, you might try for a job in the *art* department of an agency, publishing house, publicity firm, store, manufacturing company, or printing plant. Just as art courses enrich the background of a future photographer, so will an art job.

What is a typical first job?

Photography students often dream of assisting a top-notch professional for the first couple of years after school. Such jobs aren't as rare as they sound, but nor are they as glamorous as you might expect. Assisting a photographer usually means helping him carry his heavy equipment, handling lights, arranging backgrounds, mixing chemicals, keeping the darkroom and studio in order, filing negatives, processing film, retouching pictures, and perhaps helping to make prints.

You accept all these routine chores because they give you a chance to see how a professional operates. You absorb all you can, knowing that you'll never really take any pictures on such a job. You and your boss know that you'll part company as soon as you're good enough to get a job in which you *can* take pictures.

A glamor job assisting a big name photographer is *not* necessarily the ideal beginner's spot. An apprentice position in a studio, corporate photography department, or the photograhy staff of a publication will mean the same sort of routine chores; *but* you may also take pictures. These may be modest assignments at first—simple product shots, conventional portraits, nothing terribly exciting—but you might really learn more than you would learn by lugging equipment for a famous name.

Unlike most artists, photographers *can* sometimes start out doing fairly ambitious work right after they graduate. A really top graduate can sometimes skip the helper or darkroom technician stage and start taking pictures for a studio, company photo department, or magazine.

Many beginners start right out free lancing. This usually means trying to land assignments from clients *and* shooting lots of pictures on speculation. The free lance photo journalist, for instance, shoots some stories on assignment from editors; but he also does picture stories on his own and tries to sell them. Free lancing is inevitably a hectic business. It takes years to learn the ropes, to establish markets for your work, and to build up a reasonably dependable stream of assignments.

What are later jobs like?

The staff photographer, if he has what it takes, gets more and more ambitious assignments as he advances. He may have an assistant—one of the younger staffers—and may finally have a complete staff if he becomes head of a company photo department or photographic director of a publication. He may travel a lot, particularly if he's a photo-journalist. He may insist on processing and printing his own pictures, as many senior photographers still do. Or he may just shoot pictures and let his juniors do the darkroom work.

The photographic director spends a large portion of his time planning assignments for other staffers and for free lances. He oversees their work, judges the results, selects pictures, rejects others. He may actually concentrate on photo-editing: choosing and organizing photos for publication. If he organizes things properly, he can still spend a reasonable amount of time at the camera and save some juicy assignments for himself. But he's as much an editor and administrator as he is a photographer.

For this reason, many photographers reject the idea of a staff job, even one with high pay and great prestige. These men prefer to take their chances on free lancing. The successful free lance normally has a variety of clients. If he's lucky, a few advertising agencies, magazines, manufacturers, or stores will use him regularly. But most of his clients will turn up with assignments sporadically, often when he least expects them. Most free lances must invest in a studio with darkroom facilities, which they may share with a colleague to cut down expenses. It may also be necessary to hire an assistant, at least part time. This makes photography quite an expensive business.

The free lance must expect to travel fairly often. He works irregular hours, particularly if an assignment requires night shooting and immediate delivery of prints for a publication deadline. He has a lot of precision equipment to keep in working order. He may carry his own portfolio around to prospective clients or he may have an agent who sells his pictures and collects something like 25% of the price. Life alternates from calm to frenzy, depending upon the amount of work on order and the deadlines that must be met.

Many free lances resolve that they'll work alone and take only as many assignments as they can handle. But other free lances are delighted to see their business mushroom into a studio, with a staff of photographers, darkroom technicians, and even salesmen. The head of a portrait or commerical studio, like a photo department director, has heavy administrative responsibilities. He must direct his staff, deal with clients, and take pictures too, if he has time. He has the profit and excitement of running his own business, but these are balanced by the burdens of running a small corporation.

Where can you get more information?

Three popular magazines cover photography for a combined audience of professionals and amateurs: *Modern Photography, U. S. Camera,* and *Popular Photography*. Mainly for professionals are *Industrial Photography* and *Infinity*, the widely respected magazine of the American Society of Magazine Photographers. *Aperture* is a handsome scholarly magazine that deserves a much wider audience than it now has. The leading photographic annuals in this country are *U. S. Camera Annual, Photography Annual*, and *Color Photography Annual*.

Photography exhibits have become widespread. Local camera

clubs have shows in most major cities. There's often outstanding photography in the exhibitions of local Art Directors' Clubs. Many museums now have photography shows. Even art galleries have begun to give space to photographs.

But the best way to learn more about the work of leading photographers is to follow the scores of magazines that carry good pictures in ads as well as in articles. Magazines like *Look* and *Life* have built their reputations on photography. Fashion magazines like *Harper's Bazaar* and *Vogue* are also noted for their pictures. *Holiday* is well known for travel pictures. *Fortune* carries outstanding industrial photography. Scan your newsstand for dozens of other magazines that may be worth watching.

13

Art teaching

In one sense, the most important art profession of all is art teaching. For it's the teacher's job to discover and bring forth the hidden potential of the future artist, designer, or architect. Equally important, the art teacher trains the *art public*. He builds an audience for art by training laymen to understand and enjoy what the artist creates.

What does an art teacher do?

What subjects you teach depends upon *where* you teach. In a primary or secondary school, you'll probably be expected to teach a wide variety of subjects. Particularly if you're the only art teacher in your school, which often happens, you may teach any art subject under the sun. In the same class, you may teach drawing, painting, sculpture, ceramics, fabric design, stage design, fashion illustration, and perhaps even more. However, if the school is big enough to support more than one art teacher, then you may be able to specialize in a few favorite subjects, though you're still likely to carry a diversified teaching load.

Teaching in an art school, college or university art department is usually far more specialized. Painters teach painting, drawing, perhaps some printmaking if they *do* prints. Architects teach architecture, drafting, perhaps some experimental design. You don't stray from your professional field, unless you're unusually versatile.

Whom do you teach? Children and teenagers are the public school teacher's main audience, of course. But many public school systems now have adult education programs—usually in the evening—in which many students are the same age as the teacher, even older. Age limits have broadened in art schools, colleges, and universities. Though the typical student in such a school is in his late teens or early twenties, many professional art schools now have children's classes, and adult education programs for older students.

Your students may be hobbyists *or* future professionals. Public school art programs are rarely planned for the future professional. Their purpose is to introduce students to the enjoyment and understanding of art, even when programs include professional-sounding subjects like fabric design. In many large cities, there are high schools that give real pre-professional courses, but the mass of public school art students will never become professional artists.

The four year programs of most art schools are planned for the future professional. College and university art programs may be for professionals, but many are planned only for the advanced amateur, or as part of the student's general education.

As a teacher, you make your living by talking. You talk to *one* student as you look over his shoulder and criticize his work. You lecture to a class of twenty or thirty students. And you may address an auditorium crammed with several hundred students and teachers.

But for an art teacher, words are never enough. You must be able to pick up a pencil, a brush, or a modeling tool and *demonstrate*. This means that you must be a skilled artist, designer, or architect in your own right. For this reason, some public schools and *most* art schools, colleges, and universities schedule teachers' working hours to allow free time for creative work in the teacher's own studio or office.

Classroom duties aren't the only way a teacher earns his salary. There are the inevitable committee meetings to plan programs, to solve administrative problems, and to find ways of helping students who may be having trouble. There are special events: conferences and exhibits to be organized; school plays that need sets and costumes designed; social events that need decorations. There's paper work at registration and examination time. You may have office hours for private meetings with students who need guidance. And there's always the job of grading student work.

Public school teachers usually get the summer off, but there *is* a trend toward year-round school sessions. More and more art schools, colleges, and universities have summer sessions too. This means that some faculty members work the year round, which means more money but less vacation time, though there are still vacations between terms, and a lot of holidays.

Where does an art teacher find work?

As I've already indicated, most art teachers work in primary schools, junior and senior high schools, art schools, colleges, and universities. But there are also many art teachers employed in adult education schools, educational divisions of art museums, community centers, YMCA's, YMHA's, settlement houses, vocational rehabilitation centers, and even mental hospitals where art is taught for its therapeutic value. Many artists also conduct classes in their own studios.

Art teaching is certainly the most decentralized of all art professions. Though not every primary or secondary school has an art teacher, there are jobs in every major public school system in *every* state. There are also college and university jobs in every state. Nearly every major city has an art school and a museum that may offer art classes. There are job possibilities practically everywhere.

But it's vital to keep in mind that *jobs aren't equally good everywhere.* Many public school systems are ill-equipped for art teaching and pay so badly that it's facetious to talk about "job opportunities" in such places. There may be jobs, but they can hardly be called opportunities. Some states invest more in their art programs than others do. Wealthy communities can obviously invest more money in art programs than communities that aren't so lucky.

In general, opportunities for art teachers are best in fairly sophisticated cities and their suburbs. Some notable exceptions are the colleges and universities that have made a special effort to build ambitious art programs in out-of-the-way places. And the quality of many rural schools has risen rapidly in recent years. But the fact remains that the greatest number of good jobs are in cosmopolitan centers and communities nearby.

What does an art teacher study?

Leading art schools, college and university art departments offer special programs for teachers, usually called art education or teacher training. These programs are planned for teachers in *public* primary and secondary schools, but *private* schools generally get their staff members from the same programs.

Public school teachers are certified, which means that they take programs agreed upon by the state department of education and the university, college, or art school. Certification generally requires a thorough knowledge of several art subjects, plus a reasonable acquaintance with many others. Your own preferences, the school you choose, and the requirements of your state will determine which art subjects you choose for your specialties, and which ones you know casually.

Painting, drawing, and printmaking get a lot of attention in most teacher training programs. So do sculpture and ceramics. There's often a lot of time given to crafts like jewelry and metalwork. Courses in design fundamentals often lead into applied art subjects like fabric, interior, graphic, and industrial design, even architecture. Stage and fashion design are popular. Illustration may be part of drawing and painting, or it may be merged with graphic design under the heading, commercial art. Art history is always a must. Mechanical drawing is common and photography appears more and more frequently.

The bigger the art school, college or university art department, the more subjects you can study. Because primary and secondary school teachers are expected to teach a wide range of art subjects, their training *must* be diversified. However, art educators are aware that one man can't develop *real* skill in every art subject. The trend is toward greater specialization. Though training remains diversified, many schools require *real* professional competence in at least one field. The trend is away from the hopelessly diffuse training that many teachers have suffered through.

Courses in education are considered just as basic as art classes. These usually include the philosophy and history of education, educational psychology, educational theory, and individual research in educational problems. There are also specialized *art* education courses: art teaching methods for elementary and secondary schools, philosophy of art education, ways of using audio-visual aids, art education research.

Among your most important courses will be student teaching, which means going out to observe experienced teachers in action, then teaching full-time for at least six weeks.

Since a good teacher must have an exceptionally well rounded education, teacher training programs are always heavy on required courses in the liberal arts and the sciences. Required courses include subjects like English composition, public speaking, literature, history, a foreign language, philosophy, mathematics, psychology, sociology, plus other sciences like biology, chemistry, geology, astronomy, and physics. You won't be forced to take *all* of these, but you'll take a fair number. You may also be obligated to take courses of local interest, such as the history of your state.

Educational requirements for teaching jobs in art schools are more flexible. Naturally, an employer will be interested in where you went to school and what you studied. Hopefully, you have a strong educational background in the subject you hope to teach. If your schooling was rich in the liberal arts and sciences, so much the better. But there's almost never a *list* of educational requirements that *must* be met, as there is in a public school system. Art schools are interested mainly in your *ability* as an artist, designer, or architect. Your schooling counts less than your record of professional achievement.

Like art schools, college and university art departments *rarely* have a tight list of educational requirements for art teachers. Teachers' colleges sometimes insist on hiring graduates of teacher training programs, but other colleges often question the value of such training. Most colleges and universities are strongly interested in a job applicant's record of achievement as an artist, designer, or architect. However, they're also strongly interested—more than art schools—in your formal education, both in your professional field and in the liberal arts and sciences. College and university graduates are preferred. So are graduates of four or five year art school programs. For studio teaching jobs (painting, sculpture, printmaking, drawing) the Master of Fine Arts is the preferred degree; the doctoral degree is preferred for teachers of art history and art education.

An art school will often hire an artist whose education is fragmentary, who's knocked about from one school or private class to another, or just worked on his own. A college or university *might* hire this man if he had a *reputation*. But without an outstanding record of achievement in the art world, he faces tough competition from men who can point to a formal education.

Does an art teacher need a degree?

From what I've just said, it's clear that degrees are important credentials in the teaching profession.

For a public school teaching job, a bachelor's degree is essential. No major school system, anywhere in the country, will consider hiring you without a degree. Furthermore, your status and income rise with each additional degree. A master's degree automatically gets you more money and possibly a higher position. A doctorate pushes you even higher. For top administrative jobs in major school systems, the Doctor of Philosophy or Doctor of Education degree swings a lot of weight, but isn't mandatory, at least not yet.

In most states, four years of study lead to a bachelor's degree and certification. Some programs now take five years. A master's degree requires at least a year's additional study. A doctorate requires at least a couple of years more. If you're teaching full-time and just working on an advanced degree part-time, a master's may take several years and a doctorate can often stretch out to eight or ten years. Both these advanced degrees combine classwork and independent research, culminating in a sizable piece of writing called a master's thesis or a doctoral dissertation.

Art schools rarely *insist* on a degree, but they're pleased when a faculty member has one. But even here, the trend toward degrees is gaining momentum. More and more art schools grant degrees and this obligates the schools to hire teachers with degrees. Years ago, our leading art school faculties included only a handful of men with even a bachelor's degree. Now bachelor's degrees are common, and more and more art school teachers have master's degrees.

College and university art departments prefer faculty members with a formal education, as I've said, which means a bachelor's degree is a minimum requirement. A master's degree definitely improves your job prospects. Few artists, designers or architects go on to a doctorate, so a college or university can't *insist* on this advanced degree. But department heads are often expected to hold the top degree. In fact, some colleges and universities have ruled that no one can become a department head or even a full professor without a doctorate. In such schools, an art teacher must remain an associate or even an assistant professor because he lacks the label of doctor.

This obsession with degrees has forced many of our finest artists—who often have no degrees at all—to teach in art schools, rather than college and university art departments. This is a major reason for the low level of art teaching in many colleges and universities that hire men for their advanced degrees, not their talent.

What part-time and summer jobs are good experience?

The nation's summer camps have become a training ground for future teachers. For a future art teacher, the best possible spot would be the job of arts and crafts counselor. Almost every camp has one. However, if you can't be an arts and crafts counselor, any counseling job is excellent teaching experience.

You might also look into summer job opportunities as arts and crafts director of a resort hotel. There are sometimes jobs of this sort in city sponsored recreation programs conducted in local parks and playgrounds.

Throughout the year, there may be part-time counseling jobs open in community centers, settlement houses, recreation programs of churches and synagogues, YMCA's and YMHA's. In such a job, you may assist an experienced teacher or you may be given your own group of young people to work with.

A teaching or counseling job isn't the only part-time or summer experience that may be useful. If you're a skilled artist, you might land some other kind of art job. Skim back over the preceding seven chapters for ideas about jobs in other art fields. Any job that makes you a better artist makes you a more effective teacher.

What is a typical first job?

In teaching, unlike most art professions, there's no real apprenticeship period, aside from your student teaching when you're in school. When you land your first job, you start right out teaching. You're in full charge of your classes, though you may be responsible to a department head or to the head of the school. In some schools, you plan your own curriculum, while other schools give you a program to follow. But the organization of each class hour is really up to you. From the very beginning, you're your own boss.

Teaching in an elementary, junior, or senior high school, you will probably average five class hours each day. This means that during a week you may have 350-400 students to teach and grade. Getting to know this many students is no small task.

Your teaching schedule in an art school, college, or university may not be as heavy. Classes are often longer, anywhere from an hour to an entire morning or afternoon, but you may not teach a full day or even teach every day. Good art schools, colleges, and universities try to arrange your schedule to allow time for outside work in your own studio or office. Your week may include half days, a free day, or even two free days if you're very lucky.

Beginning teachers are often asked to handle beginners' classes: freshman art classes in high school; foundation year courses in an art school, college, or university. However, there's no reason to believe that introductory classes are less fun to teach than advanced classes. Many teachers feel that freshman and sophomore classes are *more* challenging just because students know so little at that stage.

What are later jobs like?

Advancement in primary and secondary school teaching is often invisible, though very real. You start out teaching and you simply go on teaching, doing a more mature job, gaining deeper satisfaction, and earning more money as the years go by. Unless you shift into administrative work, you probably won't move into a more luxurious office or get an impressive title. You may be given more advanced classes to teach as you gain experience. You may have more freedom to experiment in your classes. Aside from the bigger paycheck, your advancement consists mainly of intangibles: the respect of your students and colleagues, greater creative scope, and your own sense of achievement.

Many successful teachers in primary and secondary schools *do* move into administrative spots. They become department heads; supervisors of art programs in a group of schools or for an entire school system; even principals, the top job in an elementary, junior, or senior high school. In some administrative jobs—head of a high school art department, for example—

you may do almost as much teaching as before, with the added responsibility of running the department. On the other hand, many supervisory jobs cut down your teaching hours and give you more time for committee meetings, desk work, hiring new teachers, and evaluating the work of present teachers. A principal's responsibilities are entirely administrative.

In college and university art departments, the benefits of advancement are just as intangible as they are in public school teaching, and equally satisfying. However, the ladder of advancement *is* a bit more obvious. You start as an instructor, or possibly as an assistant professor if you have a particularly impressive background. As the years go by, your title changes to associate professor, then simply to professor, sometimes referred to as *full* professor. Colleges and universities often impose a limit on the number of full professors, which means some faculty members will never reach this top grade. The biggest difference between a beginning instructor and a full professor is usually that the senior faculty member teaches more advanced classes. Senior faculty members also head departments and committees. Like administrators in public school systems, they plan programs, hire new staff members, and evaluate current staff members for advancement.

On an art school faculty, advancement may be as invisible as it is in a public school, *or* there may be a distinct ladder to climb. In many art schools, faculty members have no titles and no precise distinction is made between junior and senior members. Seniority may just mean more money and perhaps more advanced classes to teach. Lately, however, some art schools have adopted the college hierarchy of instructor, assistant, associate, and full professor. Teachers may also be promoted to department heads and other administrative positions.

Administrative work may mean greater pay, power, and prestige, but it can be a mixed blessing. If you really love teaching, you may not want to switch to administration. Top notch teachers are often rewarded by offers of administrative posts, but frequently turn them down because they prefer the classroom to the office.

In most good public school systems, art schools, colleges, and universities, advancement means *tenure*. After a certain number of years, you become a permanent member of the faculty: your job is guaranteed.

Where can you get more information?

School Arts, Arts & Activities and *Craft Horizons* are widely read by elementary and secondary school teachers. *Art Education* is the journal of the National Art Education Association, a department of the National Education Association. The NAEA also publishes *Studies in Art Education* twice a year and offers an imposing list of other publications, including two on careers; you'll find the NAEA's address in Chapter 20. The *Art Journal* is published by the College Art Association of America.

What other magazines you read depends upon the subject you plan to teach. In each of the previous chapters, I've named leading magazines in each art field. Use these chapters to make up your own reading list, based on your interests.

Certainly the best way to learn about teaching is to watch your own teachers in action. As you watch, put yourself in their shoes. Who are the teachers you admire and why? Why do some teachers inspire you to learn, while others put you to sleep? Each class hour is a new opportunity to learn about your future profession.

14
How much
do artists earn?

One September day, a woman stepped into my office with her teen-aged son in tow and announced: "I want Harold to take a course in free lancing." "What do you mean, free lancing?" I asked. "I don't know," she said promptly, "but I hear the pay's good."

To a teen-aged artist living with—and *on*—his parents, finances may seem a rather distant problem as long as he has a bit of pocket money. But Harold's mother *had* put her finger on a fundamental requirement of any profession: the job must pay a living wage. Having explored the nine most important art fields, we now must deal with the hard boiled question of money. How much do artists earn?

Reliable income figures for artists, designers, and architects are hard to find. When you do find such figures and put them into print, your information may be outdated before the ink dries.

Artists' incomes fluctuate more than you might think. In the industrial design field, for instance, I once watched beginners' salaries shoot sky-high, drop far back, then move upwards again, all in less than four years. Why? Fluctuations in the economy had something to do with it. So did fluctuations in the number of young designers looking for work. Similar ups and downs seem to occur in most art professions.

Nevertheless, this book would be incomplete without some estimate of the earnings you can hope for as an artist, designer or architect. With the warning that no figures are reliable for very long, I'll try to suggest some salary goals that *seem* realistic at the time I'm writing this.

Fine art

Since there's no such thing as a *steady job* producing fine art, it's impossible to quote salary figures as one might for a field like architecture or graphic design. As I explained in Chapter 5, most fine artists earn their living in teaching or in some applied art job. In the next few pages, we'll look over salary prospects in these fields. But at this moment, we must still deal with the question: what do fine artists earn from the sale of their work, even if this isn't their main source of income?

So far as I know, no one has compiled accurate figures on the average incomes of painters, sculptors, and printmakers. But as I said earlier, artists generally accept one bitter fact of life: not one artist in a hundred—including artists of national reputation —can live entirely by the sale of his work. Among the scores of artists I know, the best of them hope to make just a few thousand dollars a year from sales of paintings, sculpture, and prints—if they're lucky. Many refuse to *count* on making a cent and regard a sale as a happy accident. They paint or sculpt or draw for the pleasure of it and hope an occasional sale will cover the cost of frames, canvas, paper, or clay.

Yes, there *are* fine artists who hit the jackpot and live on a five figure or even six figure income for a while, as long as their work stays in vogue. But the lucky ones are terribly rare. Furthermore, they all know that public taste changes quickly and that the jackpot can suddenly disappear into thin air. For every artist who's *now* riding high, there's another who *once* rode high.

Prices of fine art are hopelessly unpredictable. I've seen big paintings, roughly equal in size and quality, tagged anywhere from $100 to $10,000. In theory, the zeros on a price tag grow with the artist's reputation. But some well known artists keep their prices down to encourage sales, while little known artists may try to impress the public with high prices.

In the world of fine art, pricing is a matter of guesswork. Purely by trial and error, you try to discover how much the public is willing to pay for your work and what price tag will drive purchasers away. For lack of a foolproof pricing yardstick, cautious artists suggest that you begin low and hope the demand for your work will force prices up.

Beginning salaries in applied art

The Bureau of Labor Statistics of the United States Department of Labor says that beginning commercial artists—which means illustrators and graphic designers—average around $85 a week. Photographers, interior and fabric designers seem to start in roughly the same salary range. Outstanding graduates sometimes start as high as $100.

Industrial designers and architects get the highest starting salaries in the art field. The Bureau of Labor Statistics says that architectural school graduates can start at $90 to $120 a week. Industrial design graduates from top schools can start in this same range.

Later earnings in applied art

Within a few years, staffers with proven ability can expect paychecks ranging from $125 to $150 a week. They may also get an annual bonus that can go as high as a month's salary. Or a profit sharing plan may give them a stated percentage of the profits at the end of each year. Some profit sharing plans are a mere gesture, but others can mean a month's salary or even more.

Toward the top of the ladder, an art director, senior designer or design director, photographic department head, or senior architect can hope for a salary of $10,000 to $15,000 a year. Salaries of $20,000 are becoming more and more common among top men. An annual bonus or profit sharing plan may bring the total higher. And if the artist becomes an officer of the corporation—an advertising agency vice president, for instance—his annual bonus or share of the profits may some day go as high as his salary.

The earnings of a mature free lance are harder to gauge. Some mediocre free lances scrape along on $5000 a year and stay there. But a mature, successful free lance can except to earn $10,000 to $15,000, perhaps even $20,000.

The figure may go higher if a free lance practice mushrooms into a big studio operation, something that's almost inevitable in fields like architecture or industrial design, where an active business demands a full scale staff. The figure may also go higher for big name artists, designers, and photographers who remain a one man business, but collect $1000 or more for an assignment. No one knows what the big money makers earn, but some incomes are reputed to hit $50,000 to $100,000 a year, perhaps more.

Bear in mind, though, that the free lance has the heavy expense of running his own business. Thus, his income may not be as impressive as it sounds. I know one young architect who has so many clients that he keeps a staff of six working overtime, yet his weekly outlay for salaries and other overhead keeps his *personal* income down to $15,000.

Keep in mind, too, that, that no one guarantees that you'll climb the ladder steadily from a beginning salary of $85 a week to an ultimate income of $20,000 a year. Most artists, designers, and architects stop somewhere midway and climb no further.

Teachers' salaries

Nationwide criticism has forced teachers' traditionally low salaries upward, and salaries will probably go higher in the years ahead, as the teacher shortage grows worse and the public outcry becomes louder.

The median salary for beginning teachers in public schools is around $5200 a year. New teachers in large city schools may get a few hundred dollars more. In rural areas, they often get considerably less. Public secondary schools generally pay a bit better than elementary schools.

Actually, this *beginning* salary range compares well with beginning salaries in the applied art professions. It's the *higher* salary ranges that are disappointing. In the public school systems that pay *best*—New York and California—the average salary is in the $8000—$9000 range. In most states, the average is more likely $6000—$7000. A teacher does get beyond this range if he becomes a principal or a top administrator in a school system.

In most public school systems, elementary and secondary school teachers get automatic salary increases each year. These increases can be as slight as $50 but may go as high as $300 or $400 in major school systems. At some point, you approach a maximum salary and these automatic increases taper off or stop. To hold onto good people, school systems are tending to give *bigger* automatic increases *earlier*. But too often this just means that your raises stop sooner because you reach your maximum salary more quickly.

College and university teachers' salaries have risen sharply in the past few years. According to the National Education Association, the median salary is now over $9000. The median for instructors is roughly $6800; for assistant professors about $8700; for associate professors, $10,000; for professors, $13,000.

Art school salaries have never been surveyed, so far as I'm able to determine, but they seem to be less than college and university salaries. Art school teachers rarely get beyond the salary range listed for associate professors. Only a tiny handful of art school faculty members reach the salary range for professors. As more and more art schools achieve the status of colleges—granting degrees and winning accreditation—there's a chance that salaries will rise.

It's also fair to point out that teachers do get better fringe benefits than most of us: contracts and tenure mean exceptional job security; medical and retirement plans are practically universal.

Methods of payment

Artists, designers, and architects who work 9-to-5 for someone else normally get a paycheck each week or twice a month. You may get an annual bonus around Christmas. Your check from the profit sharing plan may come at Christmas or early the following year, when the past year's profits have been added up.

Teachers are always salaried unless they conduct private classes in their own studios, for which they usually charge by the hour or by the session. School paychecks usually come once a month. Since the school year is normally nine or ten months, you may get your annual salary in nine or ten monthly payments. Some schools, however, feel that it's more considerate to make a dozen smaller payments, one each month throughout the year.

Free lance pay arrangements may be simple or quite complicated. Most often, you're paid a flat fee for each assignment. Frequently, a free lance has a steady client who wants to make a more permanent arrangement. He may ask you to work so many days a month for a fixed charge. This may turn into a *retainer* agreement, whereby the client pays a monthly or annual fee for your services, plus hourly charges for your working time, and additional charges to cover special expenses like travel.

The flat-fee-per-assignment arrangement is most frequent among illustrators, photographers, and graphic designers. Industrial designers also work on a flat fee basis, but retainers are also common. Interior designers may collect a flat fee; may agree on a retainer; *or* may charge nothing for their services, but make their profit on the furnishings they sell to the client. Architects normally collect a percentage of the total cost of each building they design.

Part Three
Finding a Job

15

Writing your resume

Your school days are over. Now for the big test: you have to find a job in your chosen field. If you're lucky, a job may await you in the files of the school's placement office. Or one of your instructors may steer you to a friend of his. If you're already in a job, you might get an offer from someone who's heard of your work. But there's no guarantee that a job will drop into your lap. I'm going to assume that you have to *hunt*.

Job hunting procedures vary a bit from one field to another. It's also true that each city has its own special problems for the job seeker. And of course the *seasoned* artist, designer, or architect isn't in the same boat as the recent graduate who's never held a job. Nevertheless, the recommendations in these four chapters should be useful to almost everyone who pounds the pavements looking for an art job.

Since the fine artist can't hunt for a *job* as a painter, sculptor, or printmaker, these chapters will mean most to applied artists and art teachers. The fine artist's problems—dealer hunting in particular—have already been discussed in Chapter 5. But since the fine artist is usually forced to take a job in applied art or teaching, he's likely to face a job hunt after all. These chapters should help him.

Why is a resume necessary?

Whether you're a seasoned professional or a complete beginner, the first step in your job campaign *must* be to write a resume. This is simply a fact sheet, usually one or two pages, that tells a potential employer the main things he wants to know about you. Few job hunters realize how vital this resume is. Yet your job campaign will be immeasurably harder without this simple fact sheet, which one employment consultant calls "the job seeker's basic weapon."

Why is the resume so important? First, because many employers won't talk to you without first seeing a resume. If you don't have one to mail to these men, you automatically eliminate lots of potential employers. Second, an employment agency needs your resume to get you interviews with its clients. Third, a resume is the only practical way to answer "help wanted" ads and reach out-of-town employers. You can't tell your story in person, so you must *send* it.

Finally, once you've landed an interview, the employer has only one way to remember you among the dozens of job hunters he may see: your resume is in his file. He may not have an *immediate* opening. But weeks later he may have one *or* he may hear of an opportunity elsewhere. Naturally, he turns to his resume file. Yours had better be there.

Facts you should include

What items go on a typical resume? No two employment counselors agree completely on the scope and sequence of the ideal resume. But the following list combines the features of the best resumes I've seen. The items are listed in the order they should following on the final printed factsheet.

(1) *Name:* Your full name, including middle names or initials. Some resumes list the last name first—Jones, John —but this seems unnecessarily complicated. Avoid the affectation of putting your degree after your name—John Jones, B.A.—as European job hunters sometimes do. No nicknames, please!

(2) *Address:* Street, city, state, and *country* if the resume is going abroad. Remember your zip code and be sure to include it: your mail will reach you faster. If you have *two* addresses, one temporary and one permanent, list both with *dates.* Your temporary address might carry the notation, "June 15 through August 15." Your permanent address might carry the words, "After August 15."

(3) *Phone number:* If you have more than one phone, perhaps one at your temporary home and one at your permanent location, list each number with the appropriate address. If the phone belongs to a neighbor, explain this and add the neighbor's name. If you can be reached by phone only during certain hours, list the hours. If you include a *business* phone, say so and indicate whether your present employer knows that you're job hunting. It's important for a potential employer to know whether you can talk freely on your business phone and whether he can leave messages.

(4) *Portrait photo:* Some resumes include a small "head shot" of the job hunter. The main value of this photo is to help an interviewer recall your face several weeks after he's seen you. The picture may help him pick you out of the crowd of job seekers. I don't think a photo is essential—it certainly makes your resume more costly—but it's an extra touch that may be useful.

(5) *Summary:* Most employers are busy. They may not have time to read every word of your resume. You'll help the reader, and win his gratitude, if you lead off with a brief paragraph summarizing your background. This paragraph takes the most significant facts on the sheet and compresses them into a few lines that read like a "situation wanted" ad in the newspaper (which I'll discuss later in this chapter). You'll need a few lines about education and job experience, though you needn't *name* your schools and employers unless they're well known. You'll

want to mention the sort of job you're looking for. And you should include your age, draft status, and whether you're willing to relocate to another part of the country. Don't worry if you repeat these facts in more detail further down the page: the reader may not get that far. A typical summary paragraph appears in the sample resume further on in this chapter.

(6) *Education:* This section should list art schools, colleges or universities you've attended. Give enrollment and graduation dates. Specify your degree or degrees, if any. List major and minor subjects, but don't list every class you took unless your program was rather unorthodox and needs explanation. Certainly include academic honors like Phi Beta Kappa, awards, scholarships, or fellowships.

Extracurricular activities are worth mentioning only if they prove professional or administrative skill. For example, few employers care that you were secretary of the Square Dance Club. But they *would* be interested to learn that you served on the committee that designed the annual student exhibition. You'll note that I've left elementary, junior, and senior high school out of the education section. High school might be worth listing *only* if its one of those rare ones specializing in art.

(7) *Experience:* List jobs you've held during school, during summers, or after graduation. Your latest job should come first, then the previous job, and so on back to your earliest. Name each employer and the city where he's located. It's helpful, but not mandatory, to give an address and phone number. If your employer's name doesn't explain the nature of his business, *you* explain it. Thus, if you worked for Smith Associates, you'll have to add "an interior design office specializing in stores." Specify the date you were hired and when you left.

List your title, if you had one, and briefly describe your duties, clients, projects, and any achievements you're especially proud of. For example, a future employer would be interested to read that you'd reorganized your department or brought in new business.

The recent graduate may have very little to put into the experience section. But even the briefest jobs—part-time jobs during school, summer jobs, small free lance assignments—are worth including if they were good experience for a future artist, designer, or architect.

(8) *Special skills:* Job hunters often have special qualifications they've never used on a job, but which might be valuable to a future employer. Can you read, write, or speak a foreign language? Someone might have clients abroad. Can you type? This could be valuable in a small office. What are your hobbies? You can never be sure what side interest might ring the bell. The weekend boat builder or sports car fan might be just right for an office specializing in transportation design. On the other hand, don't waste space listing hobbies like stamp collecting, with no visible link to your profession. Nor are vague hobbies like "reading" or "travel" much help to an employer.

(9) *Professional associations:* In many art fields, there are professional associations whose names mean something to a future employer. It's worthwhile to list your membership in groups like the American Institute of Architects, the Industrial Designers Society of America, the American Society of Magazine Photographers, the American Institute of Interior Designers, or your local Art Directors Club. Your membership tells a future employer that you're making contacts and getting to know your way around the field.

(10) *Personal:* This final section is for odds and ends of personal data. Here is the place for date and place of birth; marital status; number of children; your draft status; where you prefer to work, if you have a preference. It's not necessary to include details about health, unless you

have some physical defect that would influence your work. Nor do I think it's important to give details about religion, color, or national origin. No one ever reads "vital statistics" like height, weight, the color of your hair or eyes. Skip these.

You might add other sections if you have material to fill them. If you've done some writing, for instance, add a section for publications.

What to leave out

You'll note that I've avoided all mention of money. An interviewer will probably ask what you earned in your last job and what you *hope* to earn. But don't put these figures in the resume. If the figures in the fact sheet are high, you might scare off an employer you'd really like to work for. If the figures are low, you might not be considered for a high salaried job that you're really qualified to handle.

Another thing to avoid is the supposedly picturesque detail that many job hunters sneak in to "individualize" their resumes. You'd be amazed how many resumes announce that the job hunter lives in "the oldest brick house in Circleville" or is "three time winner of the horseshoe pitching trophy awarded biennially by the Perry Street Athletic Club."

Another sort of picturesque detail is the lofty statement of purpose that begins many resumes: "I am deeply dedicated to the cause of contemporary architecture and my professional goal is to associate myself with a growing firm to which I can contribute my enthusiasm, idealism, education, and professional experience in exchange for adequate remuneration and the opportunity to perform a creative, satisfying, and lasting service to the community and my colleagues in the field." This sort of thing may be good for a laugh, if it doesn't put the reader to sleep. But it never got anyone a job.

References are sometimes included in resumes, but I'd be inclined to leave them out. Instead, keep these names, addresses, and phone numbers handy in a pocket address book. Job hunters usually find that each employer wants different references. Some employers are particularly interested in your school record and ask for names of teachers who'll vouch for you. Other employers just want to talk to your former bosses and co-workers. Still others insist on character references: old friends and respected members of the community who'll say you are a responsible person.

There are even employers who assume that *any* reference you give them is worthless because you're certain to name friends who'll stand up for you automatically. These employers won't ask for references, but they'll go out and dig up their own sources of information.

So then, since each employer will want a custom made list of references, I think it's best to wait for the interview to give him whatever names he wants. I'd only list references in the resume if the names are so well known that an employer will immediately recognize them and be impressed.

You must remember that your resume is more than a cold collection of facts: it's a sales tool. It shouldn't read like advertising copy. Nor should it include false data merely to make an impression. But you must line up the most impressive facts you can assemble; then present them in clear, dignified, literate prose that will win a future employer's respect. This prose, I might add, will be the first real test of what you learned in your English classes.

Sample resumes

On the following pages, you'll find two sample resumes: one for an industrial designer with eight years' experience, plus two years in the army; the other for a young graphic designer just out of school. Both are one page fact sheets, the ideal length if you can cram all the facts onto a single sheet. Both have plenty of heads and subheads for the employer who skims *before* he reads.

A rather stenographic style of writing keeps sentence length to a minimum. You'll see that words like *and, the,* and *he* are dropped. Paragraphs are packed with information, but not crowded together. Plenty of lines are skipped so that paragraphs don't look dense and forbidding.

The industrial designer's fact sheet doesn't stick to the sequence I suggested a moment ago. His jobs come ahead of his education, because a seasoned artist's main selling point is his experience. His military years come next because the army gave him job experience that will interest an employer. Then comes his education, which mentions a valuable year of engineering, plus academic honors and extracurricular activities. His hobbies and special skills take very little space, so these don't need a special section. They just go into the personal paragraph.

Luckily, he can fit everything onto one page. But there would be no harm in going onto a second page if he needed more space to describe additional background. If *you* need two pages, don't be worried by the old wives' tale that employers read only one page resumes. However, it *is* true that few readers have the patience to wade through *more* than two pages.

The inexperienced graphic designer's resume turns out as long as the fact sheet of the seasoned industrial designer. She gives two addresses to indicate that she's staying with a friend or relative while job hunting in the New York area. She places schooling first, since this is the major part of her career so far. Normally, your school program doesn't need much description —your major subject tells the employer what he needs to know—but this graphic designer feels that an employer will want to know about her school's unusual emphasis on printing processes. She also has a lot to tell about extracurricular activities and honors.

She has had two good summer jobs, which she describes in some detail to prove she's had a bit of practical experience. She doesn't mention her third summer job as a camp counselor: this has nothing to do with art. The personal section mentions her father for a logical reason: he was also an artist and presumably contributed to her training.

Both these resumes are typewritten. But this doesn't mean

RALPH WILLIAM SNYDER   CONFIDENTIAL

221 North High Street
Centerville 7, Ohio

CEnterville 6-2237

SUMMARY: Now assistant to product design director, nation-
ally known appliance manufacturer. Previously job
captain on business machine, appliance, transportation
accounts for independent industrial design office.
Northern State University, B.A. in industrial design.
Veteran, Corps of Engineers. Seek supervisory position,
client contact, in design office. Willing to relocate.
Age 32.

JOB EXPERIENCE 1959-Present

Allied Kitchens Corporation, Northburgh, Indiana, 1964
to present. Assistant to Director of Product Design for
manufacturer of kitchen appliances. Coordinate design
teams developing refrigerators, ovens, ranges, washer-
dryers, freezers. Consult with marketing, graphic
design departments on packaging. Handle liaison with
design office, suppliers, sub-contractors. Reorganized
model shop for low-cost production of prototypes.

Allison, Goldman & Webb Associates, Jasper, Ohio, 1959-
1964. Advanced from junior design draftsman to job
captain, responsible to partner. Major projects:
adding machine, microfilm reader, computer tape unit
for Wilton Business Machines; electric mixer, iron,
toaster, packaging for Hilldale Electric; bus interior,
exterior for Transport Division, Standard Products.

MILITARY SERVICE 1957-1959

Corps of Engineers, U.S. Army, Fort McNab, Kentucky,
1957-1959. Engineering, architectural draftsman.
Worked on new installations: barracks, storage facilities, hospital. Designed educational exhibit.
Illustrated technical publications.

EDUCATION 1952-1957

Northern State University, University Park, Ohio, 1952-
1957, B.A. Cum Laude. Major: transferred to industrial
design after one year mechanical engineering. Minor:
sculpture. Vice-president, industrial design
fraternity. Full tuition scholarship, senior year.

Harrington Art School, Harrington, Ohio, 1955-1957.
Extension courses in photography, while attending
university.

PERSONAL

Born Columbus, Ohio, 1935. Married. Two children.
Speak German. Hobbies: photography, sculpture, building
and flying gliders. Willing to relocate U.S. or abroad.
Prefer New York area, Chicago area, West Germany, or
Holland.

ELEANOR A. RUSSO

Temporary address: 241 Holly Road
Westbrook, New York
EMerson 2-3903
(July 10 through October 5)

Permanent address: 6 Maple Drive
Green Ridge, New Hampshire
Green Ridge 4077
(After October 5)

SUMMARY: Recent graduate, graphic design, Central School
of Fine and Applied Art. Summer jobs in retail advertising, printing. Seeks beginner's job in advertising,
publishing, art studio, printing plant or related
graphic arts field. Willing to relocate anywhere in
East. Age 22.

EDUCATION 1963-1967

Central School of Fine and Applied Arts, Concord,
Connecticut. Four Year Certificate in Graphic Design,
June 1967. Course included not only diverse assignments
in design of printed matter, but experience in typesetting, offset, letterpress printing. Minors:
photography, printmaking.

Extracurricular activities: Poster designer, Publicity
Committee, Central School Student Council, 1966-1967.
Designed announcements, stationery, programs for Annual
Jazz Concert Series.

Academic honors: Lettering prize, Annual Student
Exhibit, 1966. Student Honor Society, 1967. Graduated
top quarter of class.

SUMMER JOBS 1964-1966

Fox & Mendelsohn's Department Store, Green Ridge, New
Hampshire, summer 1964. Art director's "girl Friday"
in advertising department. Designed small newspaper
ads, store posters, spot illustrations, lettering.

United Printers and Engravers, Lynnfield, New Hampshire,
Summer 1966. Graphic designer attached to sales department. Designed stationery, pamphlets, packaging,
trademarks, logotypes, for small clients of printing
plant. Prepared paste-ups for offset. Developed
knowledge of type, engraving, printing, binding.

PERSONAL

Born Bangor, Maine, 1945. Daughter of Vincent Russo,
book designer, illustrator. Single. Hobby: designing,
illustrating, and printing children's books on
hand press.

you must sit up nights, like so many misguided job hunters, banging out dozens of typewritten originals, one for every interviewer. One typing job—use just one side of the page—will do. A few dollars should pay for 100 reproductions of your original, run by a local offset printer, usually in twenty-four hours.

Some offset printers will make a plate directly from your typewritten sheet, so it's important to keep your typing sharp and clean. Other printers may use their own typewriters to retype your resume directly on the plate. The printer may have several typewriters, which may mean that you have a choice of type faces. He may also be able to reproduce your photo on the resume for a slight additional charge.

Problem resumes

The format I've recommended will fit most job hunters if it's not followed rigidly, but used with imagination. However, certain job hunters have special problems which this type of fact sheet may not solve.

What sort of resume should you write if you want to change fields? Let's say you're an engineer who wants to be an industrial designer, or you're an illustrator who wants to design printed fabrics. A straightforward list of jobs, schools, and special skills won't do. Your education and experience are in your *old* field, not your new one. Though I've warned against beginning a resume with a statement of purpose, such a statement might be in order here. You might help the reader by beginning your summary with an explanation of why you want to change fields and why you think you're qualified for a new profession.

"After six years as an illustrator, I'm convinced that my skills and interests would be better used in fabric design. My decorative drawings for children's books and greeting cards have been well received. It has been suggested that this style would lend itself to printed fabrics and wallpapers. I am keenly interested in fashion and home furnishings and have spent my spare time learning more about those fields in which fabric design plays an important part. During the past two years, I have done many experimental fabric designs and have sold four to local manufacturers. I have also taken extension courses in fabric design and technology at a nearby technical school."

At this point, you can list your jobs and free lance accounts. But don't describe each job in detail. Just pick out the aspects of the job that might relate in some way to your *new* field. The engineer might explain:

"The mechanical design of this product taught me a great deal about such human factors as comfort, ease of operation, and maintenance, all of which are essentially industrial design problems. Our engineering staff worked closely with our industrial design and marketing consultants."

The same thing could be done in the education section, where you might pick out courses that relate to your new field. There might also be special emphasis on the section devoted to skills and side interests. You have a complex story to tell, a difficult idea to sell. Don't be concerned if your resume grows to a couple of pages and your sentences become fuller, less stenographic, more personal.

A spotty job record represents another resume problem. What sort of resume is best if you've hopped from one short term job to another? You may have good reasons for "job hopping"—an uncongenial boss, a sudden cutback in business, interruptions for military service or illness—but employers are uneasy about workers who don't hold jobs long enough to build up solid experience. Your problem is to prove you *have* this experience despite your irregular professional history.

One effective way to present your case is not to list jobs, but *kinds of experience*. Let's say you're a photographer with a few short term jobs as a darkroom technician, a brief stint with an industrial photographic service, and several years of diversified free lance work. After these last years on your own, you want a long term job.

When you examine your background, you find you have good experience in black and white processing and printing, color processing, industrial magazine photography, product photography, portraiture, theatrical publicity, architectural photography, and even photo editing. Your resume ought to have a brief paragraph about your work in each of these areas.

As usual, your resume should begin with a summary, but this should also emphasize types of experience, not jobs. Toward the end of the fact sheet, you can simply list employers and free lance clients in a single paragraph headed "Employers and Clients, 1955-61." No dates are needed for individual jobs or free lance assignments.

The problem resume can take many other forms. If you have a dazzling way with words, you may *not* feel that the cold, efficient fact sheet format does you justice. You may want to write an intriguing letter instead. Sometimes a man has an idea for a kind of job nobody has ever done before, a job that has to be *created*. If this is your problem, you might want to spend the first page of your resume selling potential employers on the need for this job. Then the second page would present your professional history. I've even seen resumes that were three quarters *pictures*, one quarter text and captions.

The format of the problem resume depends on your personality and the nature of the problem. But these unorthodox resumes—letters, descriptions of new job ideas, picture stories, or whatever else you might try—must be terribly good. If they aren't really "stoppers," unorthodox resumes often end up in the wastebasket. *Most* job hunters will find it best to play safe and stick to the fact sheet format I've outlined.

However, if you're eager to produce a resume which is *different*, try to choose a format that demonstrates your professional ability. One of the most memorable resumes I've seen was sent by a graphic designer who wanted a job in advertising. His resume took the form of a handsome, full page newspaper advertisement, not only well designed, but attractively illustrated by the job hunter. The lettering was also his work. And to prove his skill as an all-round advertising man, he'd written lively copy to tell his story. Not every resume can be this elaborate, of course. But if you take the trouble to design an unusual resume, the design should be *so* good that the resume could be carried in your portfolio as a sample of your work.

Too often, the unorthodox resume turns out to be *different* but neither imaginative nor tasteful. One old chestnut—which looks like a fresh idea to a surprising number of job hunters—is the resume in the form of a press release. Job hunters sometimes carry this hackneyed idea a step further: they go to a local printer or novelty shop and order a fake newspaper page, complete with headlines that scream the job hunter's name. I've even heard of a job hunter who put his resume on a phonograph record and sent it to a potential employer. The employer was not impressed. He had no phonograph in his office and he had no intention of carrying the record home to play on his hi-fi set after dinner. Like most *gimmick* resumes, the record was ignored. Employers want to hire artists, designers, and architects, not press agents.

16

Organizing your job hunt

Most job hunts are haphazard affairs: a few phone calls one day, a visit to an employment agency, casual calls on a few potential employers, all on the spur of the moment with no particular plan. Sooner or later, you find a job. But it's often *later* and often the wrong job. This sort of unplanned job hunt can drag on for months. At last, discouraged and desperate, you grab the first thing that comes your way. Well, it's not exactly what you had in mind, but it's something.

To find the right job reasonably soon, you must organize your hunt as carefully as a general plans a military campaign. Like most military campaigns, yours won't always proceed as planned. Unpredictable things happen. But a well organized job hunt gives you a sense of direction, a sense of achievement as you cover new ground each day. You'll find the actual *process* of job hunting satisfying. Above all you'll feel more confident of finding the spot you want.

Contact list

Having put the essential facts into your resume, your next step is to decide whom you want to reach with these facts. Like any good salesman, you need a contact list: a list of people you'll want to see, phone, or write.

Who should be on this list? Most job hunters make the mistake of contacting just those people they want to work for. But many job offers come from unpredictable directions. If you contact only employers who interest you, you cut out many unforeseen job opportunities that *might* be just as good.

The first lesson in job hunting is that *everybody* in the field should know you're looking. If you're an interior designer, every department store decorating department, furniture store, decorating shop, interior design and architectural office in town should know you're hunting. True, most of these people won't have jobs for you. You may not *want* to work for many of them. But there's an old saying: "Everybody has an uncle." The man who has no job for you *may* have a friend who needs you. The more people who know you're looking, the better your chance of stumbling on an unexpected opportunity.

Your most obvious source of names, addresses, and phone numbers is the classified phone directory. If you're hunting out-of-town—by mail or in person—your local phone company may have out-of-town directories. Professional organizations often make membership lists available to job hunters. If you're a graphic designer or illustrator, for example, try to get the lists of the Art Directors Clubs in cities where you want to work.

One important source, often neglected, is your personal address book. You should certainly contact your friends, co-workers, and former teachers. They may know of jobs. They can also suggest names to add to your contact list. And they may have job hunting lessons to pass on. Don't be embarrassed to ask friends for help and advice. They'll be flattered.

Professional magazines in your field are a good source of names. Read these magazines regularly to learn who are the leaders and who are others to watch. The magazines will also give you some idea of the kind of work each man or organization does. This will help you decide which employers might want your type of education and experience. For example, if you're an architect with a special interest in schools and hospitals, it's helpful to read architectural magazines to see which offices specialize in these fields.

It's simplest to put your contact list on index cards, one

name to a card. The standard small index card, three by five inches, fits the pocket perfectly, so that you can carry your contact list wherever you go. Each card includes the name of the man you want to reach, his title or function, the name of his firm, his address and phone number. You also have space for notations: Who steered you to him? Did you write to him? Did he answer your letter? Did you talk to him on the phone? Did he interview you? Did anyone else in his office talk to you? What were their comments on your background and portfolio? Did they steer you to any other contact in another firm? All these notations should be dated.

If you assemble your contact list in the way I've suggested, you may end up with a hundred or more index cards. These contacts may be scattered half way across the country. Obviously, you can't just go and see them all. Yet you should try to reach every one of them somehow. Your goal is not only to spread the word, but to land as many interviews as you can get. Each interview *could* turn into a job offer, or at least give you a lead.

There are six ways of landing that all-important interview: through a personal introduction, phone call, or letter; by answering a "help wanted" ad or placing a "situation wanted" ad; or through an employment agency. You should be prepared to try each of these channels.

Personal introductions

When you write or phone an employer, it's enormously helpful if you can say, "Joe sent me." If only out of friendship for Joe, the employer has to interview you. Besides, he may respect Joe's judgment: Joe probably sent you because he thinks you're *worth* seeing. He may even have sent you to fill a current opening.

This is known as the grapevine method. A sends you to B. If B doesn't have a spot for you, he may still send you on to C. Somewhere down the line a job is waiting for you, though you're never sure where. This sounds like a pretty rambling way to look for work. You're sent to all sorts of people who may not interest you. Most of your interviews turn out to be cordial chit-chat rather than job offers. These interviews are often pleasant, but you may wonder whether the grapevine is leading you anywhere. The amazing thing is that the grapevine method *does* work. A job materializes when you least expect it. Personnel experts often say, "The *best* jobs come along the grapevine."

The grapevine begins in the pages of your personal address book. All you need are two or three people to start the chain: a couple of friends in the field who'll introduce you to some of their associates; perhaps a former teacher who'll send you to a few employers who take a special interest in graduates of your school. The one important rule is that you *must* keep adding links to the chain. You must try to get each person you meet to send you to one or two others. You must be bold enough to ask: "Is there anyone else you think I ought to call on for a steer?"

Don't expect your interviewer to make a phone call or dictate a letter of introduction, though some do, but he might come up with some names you can add to your index cards. It's considerate to ask: "May I say you suggested I call?" If you *can* use his name, that's all the introduction you need. Even if you *can't* use his name for some reason, he's still added a contact or two to your list. You *can* call without any introduction.

Phone or write ahead for an appointment. Never just drop in without advance warning. You'd be astonished at the number of job hunters who wander in during the busiest part of the day, with the sheepish explanation, "I just happened to be in the neighborhood with my portfolio." This marks you as rude and disorganized. The employer *might* see you if he's good natured, but he has every right to throw you out.

If you phone ahead, you may be asked to send a resume and then call again for an appointment. Don't be insulted. Your interviewer wants to know more about you so he can talk to you more intelligently. If you write for an interview, instead of phoning, be sure to enclose a resume.

Phone calls

You certainly won't be able to get an introduction to everyone on your contact list. But you can still phone for an appointment. If you're trying to reach a busy man in a large organization, speak to his secretary and ask her to arrange an interview.

So far, I've assumed that you know the *name* of the man you want to reach. But what if you know the organization, but not the man? In that case, it's simplest to phone the personnel department. In a large organization, you might be routed to one of several interviewers. In a smaller place, there may be no personnel department, just one man who is responsible for talking to job hunters. In a large, highly departmentalized organization, it may be best to ask for the head of the department where you want to work. If he doesn't do his own hiring, then he'll steer you to the personnel man.

One warning about phone calls: don't just say, "I'm looking for a job." Be ready with two or three short sentences, explaining who you are, what kind of work you do, and when you'd like an appointment. A simple introduction would be: "I'm Edwin Wolf, a fabric designer with a degree from the Institute and two years' experience. Might I show you my portfolio sometime next week?" If you're in town for a just a few days, say exactly how long. Don't expect *everyone* to grant you an interview. Some will, some won't. You may be asked to send a resume and phone again. When you land an interview, it's considerate to send a confirming note. The note might simply say:

"This is to confirm our appointment on Monday, April 3, at 11 A.M. I look forward to meeting you. Thank you for your interest in my work."

Closing with the stock phrase, "yours very truly" sounds archaic nowadays. So does "sincerely yours," though many letter writers still use it. "Cordially" sounds a lot more friendly. I might add that "kind regards" is suitable *after* you've met someone and hit it off with him; it's an especially good closing for a thank you note.

Letters

You can't reach everyone by phone. Out-of-town contacts are logical targets for letters. Local contacts should also be made by letter if they're hard to reach by phone or if there are so many that you can't possibly phone them all.

If you've made up the extensive contact list I've recommended, you probably have dozens of letters to write. Job hunters in big cities like New York and Chicago often find themselves turning out a hundred letters or more. How can you cover all this territory, get all these letters into the mail, without turning the project into a backbreaking chore?

This is a time when you're grateful for a good resume. Since the essential facts are in your resume, you needn't repeat them in a letter. All you do is clip your resume to a brief note. The note must be typed, of course, not hand written. But you have only a few sentences to type, an envelope to address and the job is done.

You needn't wrack your brain composing a fresh note to go with each resume you mail. You can simplify your mail campaign if you develop a few standard messages. You can then pick the right one for each employer. Let's say you're a graphic designer with a diversified background in advertising, packaging, and magazine layout. You'll need one standard note for advertising agencies and the advertising departments of corporations; another note for manufacturers of packaging and design offices specializing in packaging accounts; a third for employers in the publishing field. Each note might be written in two versions: one for local and one for out-of-town employers.

What should your note say? Since your resume carries the complete story, all you need are a few sentences similar to your phone introduction. Your note should start off with the simple statement that you're looking for a job. Then give a few high points of your background, details that will be relevant to this particular man. Finally, you should indicate when he can meet you and see your work.

"After four years as an art director at Clark Advertising, I am interested in moving to a new job with a similar organization.

"The attached resume describes a fifteen year career in advertising and editorial art direction, with substantial free lance experience in packaging. As you will see, many of my major accounts have been in the food field, which I believe to be one of the main interests of your agency.

"I plan to be in your city on a business trip from Monday, November 3, through Friday, November 7. I would appreciate the opportunity to show you my work sometime during that week."

This five sentence note will do very well for an advertising agency specializing in the food field. The same job hunter, writing to an agency with a strong interest in packaging, might emphasize his packaging experience in the third sentence. He might also have to alter the dates in the final paragraph. But the rest of the note can be used more or less intact for all advertising agencies. His other two standard notes can follow the same basic form.

The second paragraph demands some slight knowledge of the organization you're writing to. If you've gathered your contact list carefully you *will* know something about many of your contacts. But if you don't know enough, you can still write paragraph two to fit the *type* of organization. For example, if the graphic designer who wrote the above letter didn't know the agency specialized in food accounts, he might still use his second paragraph to emphasize the breadth of his experience.

"As you will see, my advertising agency background has brought me into close contact with clients manufacturing a wide range of consumer and industrial products, both here and abroad."

The beginner, just out of school, hardly has this impressive professional history to write about. However, you *can* call attention to your special interests, summer jobs, and school projects.

"This June, I will receive a bachelor's degree in architecture from Northern State University. I am sending you my resume in hope that there might be a place for me in your office at that time.

"As the resume indicates, my most ambitious school project was a multi-story office building, designed to meet the complex requirements of this city's west side business section. My summer jobs have also included work on multi-story buildings, as well as some contact with city planning.

"I would be glad to show you my portfolio whenever you find it convenient to see me."

This note is for architectural offices with a major interest in big city office buildings and city planning. The same job hunter may have training and summer experience in residential architecture. This would be spotlighted in paragraph two of the note he sends to architects who specialize in houses.

Short notes like these can be banged out on a typewriter in ten or fifteen minutes; less if you're a good typist. You can easily turn out half a dozen each evening. Over a few weeks, you'll have a sizable mail campaign under way.

To whom should your letters be addressed? If you have a specific person on your contact list—a department head, personnel director, or even the head of the organization—there's no harm in addressing your letter to him. But don't be surprised if he routes your letter to someone down the line, who does the preliminary screening of job hunters.

If you *don't* have a man's name on your contact list, just the name of an organization, it's best to address your letter to the personnel department. If you can find out the personnel director's name, so much the better. But don't spend hours tracking him down. He won't be slighted if your envelope simply says, "Personnel Director," and your letter begins, "Dear Sir."

Don't expect everyone to answer you. They all *should*, but not everyone is polite. Some of your letters will go right into the trash basket. Others will be filed for future reference, but not answered until there's a job opening, perhaps months later, long after you've found your job. Some considerate employers will send you a polite, "Sorry, no openings." A reasonable number will want to meet you as a matter of interest. No job opening at the moment, but they'll want to remember you if they're impressed. A *small* percentage of employers will want to see you because they have a current job to fill.

Don't be discouraged by the low percentage of favorable replies to your mail campaign. You're like a general planning a bombardment. You assume most of your shells will miss, but if your barrage is heavy and well planned, a few shells will hit dead center. Remember, all you have to find is *one* job.

"Help wanted" ads

Newspapers published in larger cities often carry "help wanted" ads that announce jobs open for artists, designers, and architects. Some job hunters mistakenly assume that these ads cover *all* the jobs available. Actually, only a small percentage of current openings are advertised. Not every employer believes in classified advertising. Many just rely on the grapevine and their resume files. It's worthwhile to read the classified section and answer the ads that seem to fit your qualifications. But don't spend *all* your time answering classified ads. "Help wanted" ads don't justify more than a small part of your job hunting time.

Classified ads often sound like miniature versions of the summary that heads your resume. They usually begin by naming the position, then go on to list the main qualifications:

"Interior designer, recent graduate. Good draftsman, renderer, for beginner's spot, department store decorating staff. Some knowledge cabinetry helpful. Opportunity. Relocate."

Apparently this job will involve a lot of drafting and rendering. The employer adds that it's useful for the applicant to know something about cabinetry, but this isn't essential. The word "opportunity" is common sales talk in "help wanted" ads. The word implies that whoever gets the job will advance quickly if he proves himself. This implied promise may or may not have any real meaning. But the sales talk reminds you that a "help wanted" ad is meant to *attract* you. Like all advertising, it can't be taken at face value. The word "opportunity" may sugar coat a low salary. It may also be a means of softening what might be a blow to some job hunters: you have to relocate. You answer such an ad the same way you conduct your mail campaign. Send just two things: your printed resume and a brief typewritten note. The note should begin by explaining where and when you saw the ad. The employer may have placed several ads in a number of papers; he's interested in knowing which ad attracted you. Then explain, in just a few lines, why you feel you qualify for the job. The employer will read about your qualifications in more detail when he gets to the resume. Finally, you need a sentence telling the employer when he can meet you and see samples of your work.

"This resume is sent in response to your advertisement in the June 1 *Dispatch*, which describes a job I feel qualified to fill.

"My interior design training at Western State College included a wide range of residential and commercial projects, with heavy emphasis on drafting and rendering. My grades in drafting were among the highest in my class. I also ranked high in my rendering classes and have done free lance rendering assignments for local design offices. Though our school does not emphasize cabinetry, I have designed and built my own furniture.

"I will be glad to supply further details in a personal interview any time after June 9."

Replying to a "help wanted" ad is always a shot in the dark. The employer may get dozens of replies and arrange only half-a-dozen interviews. Most of the replies may go into the waste basket. If the employer does write or phone you, it may take him weeks. He may be snowed under with applicants from employment agencies and job hunters who've come via the grapevine. He may be too busy to start interviewing immediately. He may just be a procrastinator. Or he may not *want* to interview anyone: he may just be collecting resumes as insurance, in case a couple of his people are planning to quit.

Many artists, designers, and architects get good jobs through "help wanted" ads, though *high level* jobs are more likely to be filled via the grapevine. Though a few papers like the *New York Times* often carry ads for top men, most classified columns are best for jobs on the lower and middle levels.

"Situation wanted" ads

We've examined classified ads written by the *employer* who's looking for talent. There are also classified ads—usually listed as "position wanted" or "situation wanted"—written by the job hunter. The "situation wanted" ad is a condensed version of the summary that heads your resume. It's a summary of a summary:

"Fabric designer, 16 years experience with manufacturers, converters. Knows fashions, home furnishings. Strong technical background. Heavy experience marketing, color research. Top contacts, U.S., abroad. Bring new business. Seeks executive position with manufacturer."

This job hunter is a heavyweight. In addition to substantial experience, he adds the bait of contacts and possible new business that he might bring in. He wants a top job. This ad may appear in the classified columns in the usual small type. Or he might feel justified in paying the extra charge for a boxed ad in large type.

For the top level job hunter, a "situation wanted" ad is often a good investment. The middle level job hunter may also get good results. The ad might be placed in the classified or the business section. The Sunday paper is usually a better bet than weekday editions: more people read it and they cover it more thoroughly. The ad might also go into a professional or business magazine. The fabric designer, for example, would be wise to insert his ad in a textile industry publication. He might also try a fashion or home furnishings trade magazine.

For a beginner or a job hunter with limited experience, the value of a "situation wanted" ad is debatable. Boxed ads placed by heavyweights are surprisingly well read, often just for curiosity's sake. But I doubt that many employers read the "situations wanted"—straining their eyes over the long, gray columns of small type—as closely as job hunters read the "help wanted" ads.

Besides, classified advertising is costly. One insertion won't necessarily do. You may need several, repeated on successive Sundays or scattered among various professional publications.

You have to land a job with a sizable salary to justify this expense.

Before you invest in a "situation wanted" ad, discuss the idea with some friends in the field. If a city has several daily and Sunday papers, one paper's classified section may be better read than the others. If there are several magazines in your field, which ones are best for your ad? Like an efficient advertising man, you must do *media research* before you spend your money.

Employment agencies

Every large city has firms that earn their living by bringing employers and job hunters together. The employer calls an employment agency about a job opening. Job hunters also come in to be interviewed and listed with the agency. When the employment agent gets a job to fill, he dips into his file and pulls out records of men and women who might fit. If he can't find suitable people in file, he may advertise the job and interview candidates. The most promising candidates are sent to the employer. If a candidate is hired, he pays a fee to the agency. Occasionally, the employer pays the fee.

Few job hunters speak well of employment agencies. The typical agency seems to be a dingy, two room office in a rundown building. No one greets you as you step through the door. You take your place on a bench or a battered chair and wait till your turn comes to be interviewed. While you wait, another job hunter motions toward a registration form you're to fill out. On the back of this form is a contract you don't understand, which commits you to pay the agent one or two week's salary, maybe more, depending upon the job he finds you.

When your turn comes, you step into another small, drab room—or behind a partition—and hand your registration form to the interviewer. He scans the form, fires a few terse questions at you. If you fit a job he has in file, he gives you a few quick details, usually *too* few, then hands you a card to take to a certain address. He makes no bones about it: he's a flesh peddler. He's not interested in you as a person. You're simply a salable object. His purpose is to sell you, as quickly as possible, to the highest bidder.

This is a bitter stereotype, I know. But the appalling truth is that this stereotype fits most agencies I've seen. A few dedicated people have opened agencies based on more humane principles. Some call themselves *employment counselors* to dissociate them from their hard boiled competitors. But now the hard boiled agents are beginning to pick up the phrase. An increasing number of employment specialists are fighting the flesh peddlers by running a totally different kind of business: the employer pays the *personnel consultant* to find the right employee by an exhaustive talent hunt and elaborate psychological tests.

So it's not impossible to find an employment agent who will treat you as a human being. If you choose your agency carefully you'll get an honest evaluation of your job prospects and good advice on your job campaign. More important, the agent will carry on *his own* campaign to get you a job if he believes in you. He may call employers who *don't* have current openings, but who might be interested in seeing you anyway. He may send out copies of your resume. He may even advertise your talents if you're a heavyweight. Obviously, he's not doing this out of pure friendship: he'll collect a hefty fee if he places you, and he hopes to win future business from you and from your new employer. But the services of the few good employment agencies are worth every cent you pay.

You can't tell good employment agencies from bad by skimming their ads in the papers. Go to friends for recommendations. If you're just out of school, last year's graduates are a good source. If you're already out in the field, talk to co-workers who've been through job hunts recently. They'll remember which agencies treated them well. They'll also know which agencies specialize in art, design, or architectural jobs.

When you've selected an agency—more than one, if you can find a few good ones—treat your employment agent with the same consideration you'd give a potential employer. Don't just walk in; call for an appointment. Explain your background briefly and offer to send a resume in advance. Bring your portfolio (more about this in the next chapter) and several copies of your resume. When he sends you out to meet an employer, be sure to call the agent right after the interview and report how things went. Don't let two agents send you to the same employer: tell your agent if someone else has already made the same contact for you.

When an agent tells you about a job opening, keep it to yourself. If you start sending your friends to the employer, you're cheating the agent out of his fee. If you trust an agent, you're morally bound to send your friends to *him*. He'll then arrange to have them interviewed for the job.

One tip: though *you* are supposed to pay the agent's fee if he finds you a job, the employer will sometimes offer to pay. Ask your agent whether there's a chance of this.

Personnel consultants operate in a different way from agencies, as I've said. The consultant is paid by the *employer* and may have a staff of talent scouts, psychologists, and other experts who find and evaluate people to fill jobs. Because consultants charge high fees, employers normally use professional talent hunters only for high level jobs. Beginners' jobs don't justify the expense. Again, talk to your co-workers about consultants likely to be working for employers in the art field. But keep in mind that this is a long shot. Unlike an employment agency, a personnel consultant won't campaign to find you a job. He fills only those jobs his clients hire him to fill. There's a slim chance that he'll be looking for someone like you when he gets your resume. More likely, he'll file your fact sheet in case one of his clients wants you *some day*.

Out-of-town trips

If you're hunting for a job far from home, you're up against a special problem. You'll have a tough time finding a job in a distant city without going there. The trip can be expensive. Your transportation costs something, and each day you spend hunting costs more. It's vital to plan out-of-town trips well in advance, so you'll get the most out of every minute.

If possible, try to have plenty of appointments scheduled before you arrive in town. Don't wait till you arrive, then waste precious days trying to set up dates with busy people who may not be available on short notice. Write letters to the out-of-town employers on your contact list, asking for an interview and specifying when you'll arrive and how long you'll stay.

A good employment agency can be especially helpful when you're hunting in an unfamiliar city. They'll have contacts you don't have, plus an intimate knowledge of the local job market. If you've found an agency you trust near home, ask them to recommend an agency in another city you plan to visit. They may even have a working agreement with such an agency: the two agents might collaborate on finding you a job. If you can't get such a recommendation, write one of your out-of-town contacts and ask him to suggest an agency in his city. When you've picked an out-of-town agency, tell them when you're coming and send half-a-dozen resumes so they can start making appointments with employers.

Out-of-town newspapers are sometimes a good source of information about distant job markets. The classified ads will give you a hint of the kinds of jobs available. Read the employment agency ads to see who handles jobs in art, design, or architecture. You may write ahead about a specific job that's advertised. If the employer is interested in your resume, he may absorb the expense of bringing you in for an interview.

When you arrive in an unfamiliar town, make sure it's easy to reach you. Your family and home town employment agency should know where you're staying, so they can relay messages by mail, wire, or phone. If there's no one to answer your home phone, it may be a good idea to invest in a telephone answering service while you're away, especially if you're expecting important calls. You might also have a friend collect your mail and send important items on to you. While you're away from home, be sure to stay in a hotel, YMCA, or rooming house where someone's always on hand to take phone messages.

Carry your temporary phone number wherever you go—

you'd be amazed how many employers get a blank stare when they ask for a phone number—and call this number several times a day for messages, while you're out pounding the pavements.

Secrecy

If you have a job and you're looking for a new one, it's usually necessary to keep your job hunt a secret from your present boss. You might be lucky and have a boss who won't resent it when you tell him, "I'd like to start looking for a new job." Some bosses will shake your hand, wish you luck, offer their help and tell you, "Stay on here as long as you like." But the natural tendency of *most* bosses is to start looking for your successor. So unless you know your boss awfully well, keep your job hunt under wraps.

This isn't easy to do, but you have to try. Be sure to tell every interviewer that your current employer doesn't know you're on the prowl. You might mention this in a postscript to your job hunting letters. Your resume can simply carry the word, CONFIDENTIAL. However, it's obvious that your secret can't be *very* secret once you've contacted several dozen employers. Some are probably friends of your boss. All you can do is keep your fingers crossed.

Free lance work

All these recommendations, so far, have been intended for the artist, designer, or architect who's looking for a 9-to-5 job. But what about the free lance, the man who works in his own office or studio? He's not looking for a salaried job with a single employer, but for assignments and fees from several employers. How does the free lance find work? In many ways, his problems are quite different from those of the man who's hunting for a 9-to-5 job. In other ways, his problems are the same.

The free lance rarely needs a resume unless a potential client asks for one. More useful than a resume is a list of past and current clients, with brief descriptions of work you've done for them. This is your record of achievement, the most powerful sales talk you can assemble aside from your portfolio, which I'll discuss in the next chapter. It's worth a few dollars to have a hundred lists run by a local offset printer. Try to stick to one page and be sure the list carries your address and phone, so the client knows where to reach you at a moment's notice.

As a free lance, you can hardly exist without a contact list. You collect these contacts from colleagues and friends; from other clients who recommend you; from the classified phone directory and membership lists of professional groups; from reading your professional and business press. Unlike the 9-to-5 job hunter, you have to keep these contacts alive year after year. You must re-contact each potential client regularly. He may not have an assignment for you today, but he might in a few months.

How do you make these contacts initially, then keep them fresh? You make your first approach in the same way as any job hunter: write or phone for an appointment. Your phone introduction or note is the same three part message: (a) what sort of work you're looking for; (b) what background you have that will ring the bell with this particular contact; (c) when he can see samples of your work. Attach a client list to your note. If you phone, send a client list with a note to confirm your appointment.

If you get a free lance assignment and do it well, you'll eventually hear from that client again. The contact renews itself. On the other hand, *you* must take the initiative and keep renewing contacts that didn't result in work. You can't insist on dropping in with the same portfolio every month. But you're justified in renewing a contact when you have some new samples. Several months after your first visit, you may phone for another appointment for a brief look at the new items in your portfolio *if* the prospective client is interested. Wait even longer before trying again. Keep up any contacts who show interest, even if they have no work immediately. If your portfolio makes a good impression, you'll be remembered and called when the right assignment comes along.

A free lance has no need for an employment agency or personnel consultant, but graphic designers, illustrators, and photographers often employ an *artist's agent* to carry their portfolios and drum up business. If the agent is good, he can develop wider contacts than you can make for yourself. After all, he devotes his *full time* to making contacts, while you have to spend most of your time in your office or studio.

The agent saves you time and energy and he's well paid for it. When he wins you an assignment, he gets a sizable chunk of the price, usually a percentage agreed upon in advance. A good agent is worth what you pay him, but intelligent, trustworthy agents with good contacts are hard to find. The few good ones often have more portfolios than they can carry. To get a first rate agent, you must have a solid record of professional achievement. He rarely handles beginners. If you're looking for an agent, ask your colleagues if they can recommend one. But before you put your portfolio in his hands, talk to other artists who've used him and find out if he's as good as he looks.

Successful free lancing isn't just sitting in your cozy office or studio, sending off your work by messenger and getting checks in the mail. You have to build a detailed knowledge of dozens of clients, how they work and what they need. You have to publicize yourself and cultivate contacts for future business. You have to develop rapid, efficient working methods, so you can meet deadlines and production schedules. You have to think about budgets and bookkeeping. You're not just a happy-go-lucky Bohemian. You're running a business, and this is something few beginners are equipped to do.

Before embarking on a free lance career, you have to know the ropes. The simplest way to learn these ropes is to work for someone else. Working 9-to-5 for a boss, you can afford to make some mistakes. Beginners are expected to fumble the ball occasionally, as part of the learning process. But once you're in your own business, you can't afford many mistakes or clients won't come back with more assignments. Most of your mistakes had better be behind you, in the half forgotten days when you worked from 9-to-5.

17
Planning your portfolio

One of your job hunting letters has clicked. An employer has asked you to come for an interview. In a couple of days, you'll be headed for his office with your portfolio under your arm. For ten or fifteen minutes—initial interviews are usually short —you'll be alone in a room with your samples and a man who may offer you a job. If you make an impression, you may be asked to show your portfolio to a *series* of critical interviewers before any offer is made.

Your future hinges on the contents of that traditional, big, black folder. In most professions, a man is hired on his personality and professional history. But employers in the art field believe only what they *see*. An artist, designer, or architect must show samples. Employers realize that your portfolio can't possibly tell the whole story. Samples can't prove you're easy to work with, for instance. But your portfolio is your *only* concrete evidence of professional ability. Though architects sometimes go job hunting without a portfolio (which I don't recommend) , this is the only art field in which it's even *remotely* possible to find a job without showing samples.

What goes into this portfolio? What's the best way to display your samples? In this chapter, I'll make some suggestions for beginners, as well as for seasoned professionals. Anyone who's been through a job hunt knows that no two employers agree on what makes an ideal portfolio. But I think it's possible to set down some general recommendations that most employers would accept.

Beginners' portfolios: what to include

You're just out of school. You have no professional experience to point to, except summer jobs. You may have hundreds of school projects piled up in your room, but which ones belong in your portfolio?

Try to put yourself in the employer's place. What does he want to know about you? Above all, he wants to know something about the *scope* of your professional training. How many different things have you done? For example, if you majored in graphic design, chances are that you've done magazine and newspaper advertisements, posters, pamphlets and magazine layouts, packages, lettering, some illustration and photography, possibly some book design. If you're reasonably competent in all these spheres, better include two or three samples of each. Even if you hope to specialize in one of these areas, don't narrow your portfolio to just one field. A future employer usually wants to survey your total background.

Having argued against a specialized portfolio for a beginner, I think most employers *do* want to know your special interests. If you're an architect with a strong interest in prefabricated housing, you should certainly give this work a prominent place in your portfolio. Special interests help an employer remember you: "Oh yes, he's the fellow who's a bug on pre-fabs." You might even be lucky and get a job with an office that's working on pre-fabs. But don't count on it.

Employers pay particular attention to a beginner's *skills and techniques*. In selecting your samples, you must not only show a wide range of *projects*, as I suggested, but these projects must display all the skills and techniques that are standard in your field. Let's say you're an industrial designer whose portfolio includes appliances, automobiles, business machines, metalware, and toys. An appliance might be documented as a series of pastel sketches, culminating in a tempera rendering. You might show photos of your clay model of a car design. A business machine might be shown in line drawings, then photos of a cardboard mock-up. The idea is to prove your skill as a model-maker, draftsman, sketcher, and renderer.

The toughest thing for an employer to judge is how well you *think*. How good are you at problem solving? What mental operations do you go through in developing your solution? He'll get the full story only if he hires you and watches you work. But he likes some evidence of your mental processes in your portfolio.

Employment experts sometimes recommend that every portfolio contain one case history, tracing a project from the earliest doodle to the final solution. This *could* turn your portfolio into a bulging suitcase, but with careful editing, you can tell your story in a nutshell. An interior designer might simply show a series of preliminary sketches for a piece of furniture, then spotlight the final design in a large photo of a scale model. Architects and industrial designers often document a project with quick-reading charts and diagrams that explain the practical reasons for the final design.

Does fine art belong in an applied artist's portfolio? Every student leaves school with stacks of life drawings, paintings, and abstract designs. But these rarely add much to a portfolio's selling power. In the middle of a batch of drafting samples, the interviewer suddenly runs into some abstract paintings which the job hunter "just couldn't resist tossing in." The interviewer has to pause over each one and say, "How nice!" even if they seem irrelevant. It's best to assume that an employer's time is precious. Stick to samples that relate *directly* to your profession.

However, you may feel that fine art samples do relate directly. A fabric designer may carry some abstract color experiments among his samples, to demonstrate his knowledge of color. Or an industrial designer might show sculpture to demonstrate his feeling for three dimensional form. In short, you *may* show some fine art if it sheds light on your potential as an applied artist. But don't include more than two or three fine art samples. This is just icing on the cake.

Thinking over these portfolio recommendations, you'll discover that a beginner's samples must prove two things to a potential employer. First, your samples must demonstrate that you're a creative thinker, an idea man capable of solving big problems *some day*. Second, your portfolio must prove that *today* you're capable of handling the routine jobs that all beginners must do.

Too often, the beginner is tempted to overload his portfolio with blue sky samples that prove his *future* value, but not his *immediate* usefulness. The young illustrator crams his portfolio with cover paintings for national magazines, but no small drawings in black and white. The photographer has a vast, poetic picture story about Mexico, but no product pictures shot in his own studio. Looking over such a portfolio, one New York art director told a job hunter: "Okay, some day you'll be a great chief, maybe. But this week I'm just looking for an Indian."

Portfolios for experienced job hunters and free lances

When he reviews the portfolio of a seasoned artist, designer, or achitect, an employer is still interested in the points I've listed for beginners: scope, special interests, skills and techniques, mental processes. But there is a difference in emphasis.

If you have some job experience, you'll find that an employer is less interested in the scope of your education and more interested in the range of things you've done on the job. When you organize your portfolio, it's important to include samples of work you've done for pay. School samples are no longer enough.

How do you get these job samples? Many former employers are considerate enough to open their files and let you take, or order at your own expense, photos of models or finished products; photostats of sketches and finished artwork; blueprints; samples; page proofs of published artwork; prints from file negatives; and occasionally an *original* piece of artwork. I might add that even if you're *not* planning to leave your present job, it's wise to collect samples for possible future use, if you can collect them tactfully.

However, you may not have access to these files because your job hunt is secret or because you're on bad terms with an ex-boss. Then you have to find some other way to collect samples. If you're an architect or interior designer, get a camera and shoot pictures of finished buildings or interiors. The owners will probably be flattered. If you're a graphic designer, illustrator, or photographer, buy the magazines and newspapers where your work has appeared. Most publishers have back issues departments and there are also back issues dealers. If you're a fabric designer, you've just got to go out and buy a yard of fabric or try to get cuttings. An industrial designer can use his camera or clip out ads featuring his products. These emergency methods may not give you perfect portfolio pieces, but they're better than nothing.

Experienced artists, designers, and architects *do* sometimes carry schoolwork in their portfolios, in addition to job samples. If you're out of school just two or three years, you may not have enough job samples to tell your whole story. Your school projects may *have* to be included to complete the picture.

After surveying your scope, the employer wants to know about special interests. Few beginners can claim to be specialists, but many artists, designers, and architects develop specialties as they move up. For this reason, employers are only moderately concerned with special interests when they see a beginner's portfolio. But they may be on the lookout for specialties in the portfolios of seasoned job hunters.

Whether you're looking for a 9-to-5 job or free lance work, your portfolio should give plenty of space to samples that show your special interests. It may be simplest to divide your portfolio into sections: one for each specialty and a "miscellaneous" section to emphasize your versatility. The free lance, of course, may become so specialized that he skips the "miscellaneous" section and devotes his portfolio entirely to one or more specialties.

Employers are always interested in your skills and techniques, but as you advance in a 9-to-5 job, these may become less important. For example, it's vital for a beginning architect, interior or industrial designer to include drafting samples in his portfolio. He'll do plenty of drafting in his early years. But fifteen years later, he may do less drafting on his job, possibly none. He may concentrate on design and let younger men do the drafting. His portfolio may still include a few drafting samples, but they're less important than other samples that prove he's an idea man.

For this reason, the portfolios of top level architects, interior and industrial designers often consist mainly of photos of finished designs. It's always sensible to include a handful of drafting, model making or rendering samples, just to prove you *can* do these things. But the interviewer is likely to assume, without being told, that a senior job hunter has these skills.

Of course, lots of 9-to-5 jobs require technical skill even when you're at the *top* of the ladder. A top illustrator in an art studio never outgrows the need to draw and handle a brush unerringly. These aren't routine chores he can pass on to an assistant. The experienced illustrator knows that his portfolio must include original drawings and paintings to prove his technical competence.

If you're assembling a free lance portfolio, the nature of your work will decide how much space to give skills and techniques. A free lance graphic designer, specializing in advertising layout, may carry nothing but proofs of printed pages. His clients aren't interested in seeing original layouts or paste-ups. They want to see the final ad. But a free lance photographer had better show *actual prints*, made in his darkroom, to demonstrate his craftsmanship.

Since teaching skill is so difficult to document in a portfolio, few job hunters even try. Yet the few who *do* try are often remarkably successful. An obvious solution is to show a diversified selection of your students' work, whether originals or photos. I've seen memorable portfolios put together by public school teachers who took a camera into the classroom to record a lively class project. The photos were combined with samples of the children's work to document the case. I also recall an art school teacher who developed an experimental method of teaching life drawing: for his portfolio, he drew a series of charts to explain his theory. These are elaborate, time consuming ways to build a portfolio. No interviewer *insists* on seeing such unique portfolio pieces. But when he does see something unique, he's not likely to forget.

Portfolios for job hunters who hope to switch fields

A few years ago, I was visited by an electrical engineer who wanted to be an industrial designer. He carried what *he* called a portfolio: a folder full of diagrams that meant very little to me, except that he seemed to be a skilled engineering draftsman. I asked if he had any art training. No, he'd never drawn or painted, outside of a few classes he'd been forced to take in high school. What were his hobbies? Did he build furniture, make ceramics, tinker with cars, try to redecorate his home or office? Did he do anything that was even remotely related to industrial design? Well, no, his only real hobby was collecting coins. All he knew was that he was unhappy in electrical engineering and "sort of thought" he might be happier as an industrial designer.

For all I know, he might have made a brilliant designer. But he had no evidence to support his case. We *might* have hired him for a year's tryout, but investing time and money in him seemed absurd when we could have a trained designer for the same salary. All I could suggest was that he stick to his present job and take night courses at a local art school to see if industrial design was really what he wanted. When he'd learned to draw and completed some classroom design problems, I'd be happy to see him again *with samples*. This seemed to discourage him. He never came back. I assume he's still griping about being an engineer.

The disgruntled engineer was typical of many job hunters who hope to switch fields. They want a new job, but they have no samples to prove their qualifications. Nor are they willing to make the effort needed to create this portfolio.

Of course, *some* job hunters have ready made samples. An architect can often use an architectural portfolio to get an interior design job. A mechanical engineer with lots of experience in product development, marketing, and human engineering—plus the ability to draw freehand—might qualify for an industrial design job. But these are the lucky few.

More common is the job hunter who has *some* relevant experience or training, but not enough. A common case is the illustrator who wants to be a graphic designer: he can fill *part* of his portfolio with drawings or paintings, but he also has to show some layouts. This type of job hunter can often fill the gaps in his portfolio by spending his spare time creating the necessary samples. This may mean months of evenings and weekends, but without these samples his job hunt will be long and his prospects dim.

Painfully common is the job hunter with *no* relevant experience. Like the unhappy electrical engineer, he has *no* samples. The logical way for this job hunter to create a portfolio is to go back to school. This takes time and money, but the investment has to be made.

If you're hoping to switch into a new field, you must remember that you face stiff competition from job hunters *already* in that field. They have education and experience that you lack. They have portfolios filled with the right samples. You must convince an employer that you're as good as the competition. At home or back in school, you must build a portfolio that can stand comparison with other portfolios that cross an interviewer's desk. If this doesn't seem worth the effort, better stick to your old job.

Some suggestions about format

The traditional portfolio looks like a huge, black file folder. Two sheets of black cardboard are hinged together along one edge and frayed shoe laces appear at various points so you can tie the whole thing together. This coffin for artwork has only two advantages: it's cheap and it's light. But anybody who's carried one will remember its drawbacks for a lifetime. After a week of job hunting, the black folder looks as shabby as an old shoe. There's no handle and no way of carrying the folder comfortably *without* a handle. When you want to untie the shoe laces so an interviewer can see your samples, the knots won't give: someone seems to have dipped them in glue. When you want to *tie* them and make a graceful exit, the knots refuse to hold and your samples spill across the floor. Humidity in the air makes the boards curl like potato chips. And heaven help your samples if it rains!

There are much better ways of carrying and protecting samples. A large accordion envelope, usually the color of decayed salmon, is just as ugly as the traditional portfolio, but easier to open and shut, and cheap enough to replace when it gets ragged. This also give you *some* protection against weather, particularly if you coat it with lacquer from a spray can. If you can afford to spend more, you can buy a large leather portfolio, something like a briefcase with zippers on three sides. The zippers are easy to open, though sometimes hard to close. But it's easy enough to throw in your samples, make a quick exit and zip the folder afterwards. If your samples aren't too big, an attaché case or briefcase will do handsomely.

When I discussed beginners' portfolios, I said employers like to see case histories to get some idea of how your mind works. In a beginner's portfolio, case histories can be powerful selling tools. They're less important in an experienced job hunter's portfolio, which includes examples of real projects—not schoolwork—successfully completed.

However, many seasoned professionals still include simple case histories. Often, these are nothing more than before-and-after pictures, showing a product before redesign, then after. An illustrator sometimes shows a few preliminary sketches, then the finished drawing or painting. A graphic designer might show alternative forms of a trademark design, leading up to the final trademark. Case histories like these aren't *essential* in the portfolio of an experienced job hunter or free lance, but they're worth including if they tell an interesting story and don't take too much space.

Portfolios for teaching jobs

The art teacher's portfolio presents a special problem. He doesn't expect his employer to buy drawings, paintings, photos, or other artwork. The art teacher is paid for a vague thing called knowledge and the ability to transmit this knowledge to students. The portfolio supplements his "credentials": his academic record, his license, and his references. The art teacher's portfolio does this in two ways: it demonstrates that the job hunter is a competent artist and suggests that he's a good teacher.

The way to prove your competence as an artist is simply to show samples of your work. If you're a *recent graduate*, your art school, college, or university samples are logical things to include. If you're a *seasoned teacher*, you've probably taught a variety of art subjects and you may not feel that you need a portfolio to prove it. Your record may speak for itself. But even then, a good portfolio has a lot of selling power.

The portfolio will naturally divide itself into two sections: specialties and other art subjects you're qualified to handle. Specialties will probably dominate, if only because they're your best samples. If your major interests are painting, drawing, and printmaking, let's say, you might include four or five examples of each. Then come your secondary interests, subjects you *can* teach, but which aren't your specialties. You'll need just one or two samples of each: perhaps a stenciled fabric; one or two photos of sculpture; a sketch for a stage set; samples of a few crafts like metalworking, ceramics, or weaving. Keep in mind that if you're going to contact school systems in different parts of the country, you may have to meet different requirements each time you're interviewed. It's useful to have extra samples on hand, so you can alter your portfolio when necessary.

Though scope is essential in a *public school* art teacher's portfolio, specialization means much more if you're hunting for a job in an art school, college or university art department. If you're a sculptor, you'll be expected to teach sculpture, three dimensional design, and probably some drawing. Sculpture and drawings are the main things an interviewer expects to see in your portfolio, though he'll be interested in seeing *some* evidence of your other interests. Art schools, colleges, and universities are always interested in *some* versatility. An interviewer might be delighted to see samples indicating that you can teach a few classes outside your main field of interest. There are plenty of graphic designers whose portfolios include photographs and illustrations; sculptors who show ceramics; architects who show furniture. However, these portfolios are rarely as diversified as the samples of a public school teacher. Specialties still dominate.

The hardest thing to communicate in a portfolio is teaching ability. Most often, an employer looks at your portfolio for proof of your art background. To gauge your value as a teacher, he depends on your record, references, and personality. Unfortunately, some interviewers assume that good samples make a good teacher and look no further. This explains the shocking number of distinguished artists, designers, and architects who get top school jobs and turn out to be mediocre teachers. Every art student has met them.

After a few years of seeing job hunters, an interviewer is prepared for *anything* when a portfolio is opened. And *anything* is what he often gets. An amazing number of portfolios contain dog-eared sheets of paper in all shapes and sizes. There are pages torn from sketchbooks; blueprints folded in devious ways and impossible to open without tearing; pencil, charcoal, and pastel sketches which the job hunter forgot to spray with fixative, so the color comes off on the other drawings *and* on the interviewer's fingers; small, out-of-focus snapshots that get left behind among the papers on the interviewer's desk; drawings on tracing paper that you can't figure out because the drawing underneath shows through. Half the samples are face down. Others are sideways. And out of the pile, when you least expect it, slips a tiny plaster model that smashes on the floor.

One designer swears that he's going to buy an electric fan and keep it going full blast on his desk: "When somebody opens a portfolio, all those loose scraps of paper will get blown back in his dumb face!"

Order is the interviewer's first requirement when he opens a portfolio. He has neither time nor patience to riffle through a stack of odd size sheets. The simplest way to create an orderly portfolio is to paste *everything* on standard size cardboards, all the same weight if possible. With all your samples the same size, the interviewer will flip through your portfolio without effort or interruption. Paste samples on just one side of a board. This makes it easy to keep boards in the proper sequence, all facing in the same direction. Several small items can be pasted on one board, if they're related, like a series of thumbnail sketches or small photos. Even color transparencies can be mounted on cardboards; just cut a hole in the board, so light can get through. The interviewer can hold the card up to a lamp or a window if the board isn't too big and heavy.

A more expensive way of doing the same thing is to buy a large looseleaf notebook in an art supply store or stationery store. These now come in enormous sizes, especially for port-folios, and contain transparent acetate sleeves for artwork. You mount samples on sheets of thick paper and slip the sheets into the sleeves. Sturdy black paper is sometimes supplied with the book. If you prefer some other color or a *variety* of colors, art materials stores usually have a good stock of draw-ing papers in various tones. Keep in mind that acetate sleeves protect artwork, but tend to get scratched up. They also tear easily, particularly at the holes where looseleaf rings come through. It's sensible to have extra sleeves on hand to replace damaged ones.

A big looseleaf notebook is luxurious, but nobody will call you a piker for using boards. In fact, boards have some advan-tages over a notebook. As he thumbs through the boards, the interviewer can set aside some samples for a second look. He can stand them against the wall and back away to see them better. And you can quickly reorganize boards, deleting some, adding others, for your next interview. All these things are less convenient when samples are under acetate in a looseleaf book. Samples are also easier to see without acetate, just as paintings are easier to see without glass. On the other hand, bare boards give your samples less protection. Try spraying the boards with plastic lacquer which art materials stores supply in a spray can.

By choosing boards or a looseleaf book, you'll make the interviewer's life easier. You'll also protect your precious samples from the crumpled, dog-eared look that dooms loose sheets of paper.

The only samples you can't protect this way are drafting

samples too big to fit into a portfolio without folding or rolling. Don't roll them. The cylindrical shape won't fit into your envelope or briefcase, so you must carry the roll separately and risk having it crushed. Worse still, rolled drawings never lie flat on an interviewer's desk. All you can do is fold them neatly and *logically*, so interviewers can open sheets quickly and you can refold them without too much fuss. Be sure to fold them all the same way, according to some logical plan, so the interviewer doesn't tear them or open them in the wrong direction.

Another solution is to make small photostats of big drafting samples. Stats are a good way to show off your designs, but the quality of your drafting may be hard to judge. If you have lots of drafting samples, you might photostat the ones that show design ability and paste these on boards or looseleaf pages. Then carry folded full size prints of drawings that show drafting skill. Big, unmounted drafting samples soon show signs of wear. Better have extra prints of each drawing.

How many samples should you include? There's no infallible answer. Some employers have more patience than others. But it's safe to assume that an interviewer has only a short time to spend with you. I don't think you should make him turn more than twenty boards or looseleaf pages. If you can tell your story in less, better still. An experienced artist, designer, or architect needs only a few samples to judge you. If he wants to see more than fifteen or twenty items, he'll ask for them. You might carry an envelope of extras just in case. But don't haul them out and flood your interviewer's desk unless he *really* wants to see more.

Job hunters sometimes number pages or boards. But they regret the numbers when they decide to add or delete samples. Better leave the numbers off. However, it's often helpful to label samples. Some portfolio pieces explain themselves at a glance. But others may need clarification. For example, it may be obvious to an interviewer that you're showing him an upholstery fabric. But he may not be able to guess the exact blend of fibers. You could *tell* him, but it's considerate to label the sample.

An intelligent label does more than just identify something.

It gives the interviewer some basis on which to judge your work. In an industrial designer's portfolio, the caption, "Power Lawn Mower," tells the interviewer something he could guess just by looking at a photo. But call the product a "Low Cost Power Lawn Mower," and you help him judge its suitability for low cost production and the mass market.

A label doesn't have to be hand lettered unless you're skilled with a lettering pen. You can buy handsome paste-on letters in an art supply store. A sharp, clean typewritten caption is also good looking and unobstrusive.

Color slides

More and more job hunters carry color slides. These *can* be enormously effective portfolio pieces, but they can also be a headache.

I once sat at my desk, grinding my teeth while a job hunter set up a suitcase full of equipment to show me two dozen slides. He spent ten minutes trying to figure out an expensive new projector he'd bought for his job hunt. Then he discovered he needed an extension cord. An office boy finally located one at the other end of the building. To set up a portable screen, we had to move my desk. At last, a tray of slides went click-click into the projector and I dimmed my lights. The first slide appeared on the screen sideways. The next four were upside down. Desperately, the job hunter tried to reverse the automatic mechanism to get his slides out and try again. The projector jammed. We smelled burning film. I pulled out the plug and suggested he come back later *without* slides.

If you're going to show slides, steer clear of projectors, screens, and other equipment that clutter up the interviewer's office. All this paraphernalia takes ages to set up and knock down, while your interviewer politely smothers the urge to throw you out. The more equipment you have, the greater your chances of a mechanical failure. You may not be invited back for another try, unless the interviewer takes pity on you.

A small, portable viewer—most of them look like tiny TV

sets—is the most convenient device for showing slides. The best kind is a desk top unit that holds a tray or a cartridge of slides that pop through automatically. A battery operated viewer is infinitely better than a plug-in model. Don't make an interviewer wait while you crawl around his floor, looking for an electric outlet.

You may have to economize and buy a hand fed viewer, one that requires you to insert and remove each slide by hand. Whether you get a desk top model or one that's held in your hand, be sure you test various models to make certain that slides are easy to get in and out.

Another type of hand viewer actually has to be held against the eye. You look into it like a miniature telescope. Interviewers who wear glasses sometimes object. I think you're safer with the kind that looks like a TV set.

Many interviewers prefer to look at slides with the naked eye. This is hard to do with 35 millimeter slides, for which most viewers are designed. But it's perfectly practical with larger transparencies. Many job hunters shoot 2¼ by 2¼ slides, which can be seen with the naked eye *or* through a special viewer. You can carry a viewer just in case and let the interviewer decide whether he wants to use it.

Slides are best for three dimensional subjects like buildings, interiors, products, packages, displays, and other samples that you can't carry. Most interviewers object to slides of two dimensional objects like illustrations, fabrics, or drafting samples. It's hard to judge your technique without seeing the original. Thus, slides seem best for architects, interior and industrial designers, not for artists who work in two dimensions.

It's difficult to put a complete portfolio on slides. A top level architect or designer might show slides just of finished buildings, interiors, or products. But most job hunters divide their portfolios into two parts: slides of models or finished work; plus a folder of sketches, renderings, and drafting samples.

Models

A nervous young man once stepped gingerly into my office,

balancing an immense cardboard box on his shoulder. He quickly announced his name, set the box on the floor, lifted out a delicate model of an exhibit and placed this carefully on the chair next to my desk. With a sigh of relief, he shook my hand,backed up to the same chair and sat down. That crunch still haunts my dreams.

Models belong in a portfolio only if they're small and tough. This automatically excludes most architectural and interior models. Industrial designers' product models sometimes fare better: wood, metal, and hard plaster are meant to take a certain amount of punishment. But if you carry product models, it pays to build a special padded box, as some industrial designers have done. Stick to small items an interviewer can hold securely: things like an electric shaver or a hand mixer. An interviewer will never forgive you if you hand him some delicate gadget that slips out of his hand like a cake of wet soap.

The safest way to show a fragile model is in a photograph. This may not do *complete* justice to your craftsmanship, but a good, sharp close-up will give a reasonable idea of your model making skill. If the interviewer asks to see the actual model—he rarely does—then you have to take a chance and bring it in. Until then, keep it safe at home.

Unusual portfolios

Conventional portfolios—mounted samples, looseleaf books, and slides—are always a safe bet. But you may not be satisfied that a conventional presentation does your work justice. If you can devise a more unusual way to design a portfolio, don't let this chapter hold you back. But don't be carried away by gimmicks, like the graphic designer who brought me a looseleaf book full of packages that popped out like a Jack-in-the-box as I turned each page. His trickiness defeated him. I can remember the gimmick, but I can't recall any of his samples.

An unusual portfolio format is worthwhile only if it's a *more logical* way of telling your story. One of the most memorable portfolios I've seen was a stack of blank index cards and a scissors. An interior designer had developed a line of furniture based on a unique principle: each item in the line could be made from a single sheet of metal, cut at several points and bent into shape. The designer felt that sketches and photos were too static to explain his manufacturing method. He was convinced that only a demonstration would do the job. He asked me to think of each index card as a sheet of metal. Taking a scissors out of his pocket, he quickly snipped a card at several points and bent it with his fingers. The operation took half a minute and was repeated till I had a complete line of furniture on my desk. He'd rehearsed the demonstration and knew it would take no more than five minutes to *construct his portfolio* before my eyes.

Another job hunter who felt the need for a less static portfolio was an architect whose major interest was trade fairs. He'd built extraordinary models of experimental displays, too fragile to bring and too complex to make sense in a *still* photograph. So he made a brief eight millimeter motion picture. The camera roamed in and out among the colorful shapes, revealing dramatic details and structural innovations. The whole movie was on a four minute film cartridge which he simply popped into a portable projector with a minimum of setting up time. Everything went smoothly. No upside down images and no burnt film. This portfolio was worth waiting for.

Not every job hunter has samples that lend themselves to demonstrations or motion pictures. Your samples must *justify* this unusual treatment. And your off-beat portfolio—like an off-beat resume—must be exceptionally good to win the interviewer's patience. Unless your samples really *demand* unorthodox presentation, think twice about departing from the conventional portfolio format.

Planning the portfolio to fit the interviewer

Before you step into someone's office with a portfolio under your arm, take another look at your samples. Chances are that you know a few facts about the man who's going to interview you. Though you may not know the man *personally*, you can probably make some intelligent predictions about the kind of samples he'd like to see. Would it be wise to delete some samples? Do you have some extras you might add?

Even if you know nothing about your interviewer except the nature of his business, you may be able to tailor your portfolio to fit his interests. Let's suppose you're a graphic designer about to visit an advertising agency. All you know about your interviewer is his name and that he's an advertising man. You don't know his agency's accounts. You don't know how the art staff is organized or what sort of talent they're looking for. But glancing through your portfolio the evening before your interview, you're reminded that only half your samples are really advertising layouts. The other half is a blend of magazine layouts, book designs, packaging, and a few illustrations. You need more emphasis on the advertising samples, less on the other kinds of graphic design you've done.

First, it's probably safe to delete most of the book designs. This isn't your interviewer's field. Are you particularly proud of *one* book? Well, leave that one in as matter of interest. Now, what about the magazine layouts? Not really your interviewer's field, but closer to advertising than the book designs. Keep a few, but delete some others. Packaging samples? More agencies are getting into packaging. Better hang onto several; just delete a few. Illustrations? You like to draw and the agency might need a good illustrator for smaller ads that aren't farmed out to free lances. Better hold onto these samples. Having trimmed down the portfolio, what can you add? Not all your advertising layouts were in the original portfolio. There are some extra samples in your desk drawer. You can certainly add some of these to bring your samples back to the original number.

You can even alter the sequence of your samples. Perhaps the magazine layouts originally came first, then some advertising samples, packaging, then more ads. Now it seems advisable to concentrate advertising samples at the beginning, then follow with packaging and magazine layouts, saving your dramatic illustrations for an "upbeat" ending.

You've really made no drastic changes in your portfolio.

Most of the samples are the same. A handful have been deleted, another handful added, and you've re-shuffled things to put the most important samples first. It's essentially the same portfolio, but with a *different emphasis*. With a few minutes work, you have a portfolio that will have *much more impact* on this particular employer. If you have a second interview that same day, it takes only a few more minutes to re-shuffle your samples again and come up with another custom made portfolio. You can carry extra samples and do your switching between appointments. You may even keep a list of each portfolio arrangement you've tried, so you can repeat a successful arrangement without racking your brain to remember the sequence.

Naturally, if you're just out of school, you may find it difficult to add or drop samples whenever you have an interview. You may not have enough samples. One set of samples will do. But after you've had a job or two, you'll have more material to choose from. Over the years, you should accumulate an arsenal of samples, so you can choose your weapons when you plan a job hunt.

18

Conducting job interviews

You'll be interviewed by many employers before you find the right job. When an employer makes an appointment to meet you, he *might* have a current job opening. If he has no current opening, he may be thinking about creating a new spot in his organization *if* he finds the right man. He may know of a spot somewhere else in town. Or he may be seeing you just out of curiosity. You can never tell. But each time you step into an interviewer's office, this *might* be the climax of your job hunt. As you open your portfolio, you always wonder if the conversation will end with a job offer.

You need more than a good portfolio and a good resume to win that job offer. The big moment also hinges on how well you conduct your job interview.

Are you surprised by the suggestion that *you* conduct the interview? Doesn't the *employer* do the interviewing? It may look that way. After all, the employer asks the questions and you answer them. But the interview is the *job hunter's* show. The employer is the audience. An intelligent job hunter knows that *his own* words and actions determine whether the show is a hit. He plans an interview as carefully as he plans his resume and portfolio.

This chapter makes some suggestions about how to plan and conduct a job interview. Though these suggestions will mean most to the job hunter who's looking for a 9-to-5 position, many of these recommendations will apply just as well if you're looking for free lance work. Whatever sort of work you may be seeking, you still must meet potential employers and be interviewed.

Twelve ways to irritate an interviewer

Interviews are often wrecked by small things. A job hunter with an impressive portfolio and resume can still ruin his job prospects by a few thoughtless acts. Here are a dozen common ways to irritate a potential employer:

(1) *Don't arrive on schedule.* Job hunters are often late. They sometimes have good reasons. The previous interview may have taken longer than expected. But few job hunters have the courtesy to phone and say they're off schedule. They just walk in late and expect the employer to see them anyway. Job hunters don't seem to realize that an interviewer's day may be tightly scheduled, allotting just so much time to each appointment. If you're half an hour late, the interviewer must re-shuffle his other dates to see you. Getting there half an hour early can be almost as inconsiderate as arriving late. He must disrupt his schedule to see you immediately. Or he's forced to keep you waiting and he's embarrassed.

(2) *Mutter your name so the interviewer never really gets it.* Then continue to talk inaudibly throughout the interview. Your interviewer will wonder if he needs a hearing aid. As you talk, he'll search vainly for the slip of paper on which he'd scribbled your name when you phoned for an interview. When you leave, he'll shake your hand awkwardly and bid you, "Goodbye, Mr. Ummm."

(3) *Get the interviewer's name wrong.* Keep calling him by this wrong name and use it in the thank you note you send the following day. Few job hunters have the foresight to double check the interviewer's name with the receptionist.

(4) *Forget to bring an extra copy of your resume.* You mailed him a copy, but this is filed, or on someone else's desk. So he's forced to hear you repeat your resume aloud. If you'd brought the resume with you, he'd spend a minute scanning the page, then move on to your portfolio. Instead, he has to spend an exasperating five minutes pulling facts out of you and trying to remember them.

(5) *Talk about everything but the subject.* A surprising number of job hunters act as if employment is the last thing they want to discuss. They'll use any excuse to avoid getting to the point. The weather is a favorite: "Boy, today's a scorcher. I was at the beach Saturday and . . ." Personalities are also a popular dodge: "Jack Doolittle sent me over. Say, have you heard about Jack's new . . ." At last the job hunter runs out of small talk and opens his portfolio with a resigned look that suggests, "Well, we had to get down to business sooner or later." By now, the interviewer's time and temper are growing short. He's forced to race through your portfolio and skip most of the questions he wanted to ask.

(6) *Dump your portfolio on the interviewer's desk without warning.* Don't ask where to put your portfolio, just drop it in front of him with a thud, scattering his papers and tipping over his ashtray.

(7) *Apologize for your samples.* Nothing discourages an interviewer more than the news that, "These aren't really my best samples. I'm still working on the best ones, so I left them home." Another common apology: "A lot of these samples aren't so hot. They're old stuff, but I haven't had a chance to weed them out." Still another apology: "I wasn't sure what you wanted to see, so I just threw everything into my briefcase." When you start an interview with an apology, the interviewer wishes he could say, "Go home and come back when you can show me your *best* samples and nothing else." But he may not give you a second chance.

(8) *Insist on turning the portfolio pages yourself,* with a detailed running commentary. Of all the ways to make an interviewer's blood boil, this is the best. Don't let *him* thumb through your samples. You do it. Linger over each sample and tell its story in encyclopedic detail: "I remember starting this job on a Tuesday afternoon. It was the first thing I'd done for this client. The client had called my boss that morning and . . ." At this rate, it may take half an hour to get through your portfolio. But after ten minutes, the interviewer will probably announce that he has another appointment.

(9) *Evade his questions.* Never give him a specific answer. Be vague and watch him grind his teeth. When the interviewer asks why you left your last job, don't explain that the staff was too small to allow room for advancement. Just say, "I wasn't happy there." If he asks how you did in school, don't tell him you graduated in the top third of your class, made consistent B's and some A's in your major subject. Just say, "Pretty well." At the end of the interview, the employer won't know much more than he did when you walked in.

(10) *Know nothing about your prospective employer.* If you want to do more than irritate an interviewer, you can really *antagonize* him by your total ignorance of his business. He doesn't expect you to know *much* about his work, of course, but he'll be shaken to find that you think he's a magazine publisher, when he's really a book publisher. You can also rattle him by admitting that you've never read any of his magazines. He may get a good laugh out of the interview. But he may also take your ignorance as evidence that you don't *care* enough about his organization to work for him.

(11) *Fiddle with the objects on the interviewer's desk.* Distract his attention from your portfolio by picking up his paperweight and rolling it about in your hand. Scan the letters

on his desk. Pick at a frayed corner of his desk blotter. He'll be so busy watching you fidget, he won't remember a word you say or a single item in your portfolio.

(12) *Forget to leave.* When the interviewer has finished looking at your portfolio and you've both asked all the essential questions, don't get up and go. Just sit there and keep talking about nothing in particular. Chat about baseball scores, politics, books you've read lately, anything to drag out the visit and waste the interviewer's time. Ignore the fact that his next guest is waiting outside. Make the interviewer get up and show you the door. Don't leave till he seems on the verge of throwing you out.

This list of irritations is no joke. Job hunters commit these small sins every day. Interviewers develop thick skins and a good sense of humor, but no one really gets *used* to inconsiderate job hunters. A thoughtless act, no matter how small, is rarely overlooked.

Your personal appearance

The need for good grooming and good taste in your clothes seems so obvious that I was tempted to skip this section altogether. But since I began *Art Career Guide*, at least a dozen colleagues have complained about job hunters' paint clogged fingernails, unshaven faces, fire engine red sportshirts, faded blue jeans, baggy plaid sport jackets, jangling jewelry, and dresses cut so low that no male interviewer can concentrate on the portfolio. So here are a few suggestions that may seem unnecessary to *some* readers, but may be helpful to others.

Theoretically, at least, we all learn the elements of good grooming when we're children—hair combed, hands and face scrubbed, fingernails cleaned and trimmed—so there's no point in going into detail here. But many job hunters must race directly from their classrooms or other jobs to an interview, with no time for a shower or a change of clothes. Under these circumstances, how can they hope to appear well groomed?

A good solution might be to make yourself a portable clean-up kit. Buy a small tube of hand cleaner if you spend your day elbow deep in paint or clay. You can buy a tiny nail clipper with a built-in file. You can also get hair cream in a tube. For girls, there are cans of hair spray and plenty of cosmetics in small packages. A soft cloth and perhaps a small bottle of liquid polish are useful for giving shoes a quick treatment. The list might go on to include things like a hairbrush, a mirror, spot remover, and anything else that occurs to you. The whole works should fit into a small box, a briefcase, or a girl's shoulder bag. I think I can safely assume that running water, soap, and paper towels will be handy somewhere in your school or office.

One further tip: if you're wearing good clothes for an interview later in the day, protect them with a smock or an apron while you're working.

Now, what about clothes themselves? What should you wear? An artist, more than most job hunters, is expected to show good taste in his clothes. This doesn't mean you must go into debt to buy a suit from the finest London tailor or a dress from a Paris salon. But it does mean that your clothes should be well cut and harmonious in color and texture.

For a man, the traditional dark suit is always a safe bet. Some interviewers *insist* on a suit, but I see nothing wrong with a sub-dued sport jacket and dark slacks. The thing to avoid is the jazzy plaid jacket that always turns up in foreign caricatures of American tourists. I'd also stick to dark shoes. In shirts, white, a subdued solid color, or a quiet stripe are all acceptable. Four-in-hand and bow ties are equally good, it seems to me, even though tradition favors the four-in-hand. You can afford to be a bit adventurous in tie colors, though I'd still avoid wild patterns and intense hues.

For a woman, a dark suit is also traditional and safe. So is a trimly tailored, dark dress. Though it's wise to dress conservatively when you're job hunting, a woman can always dress in more adventurous colors and styles than a man. If you're looking for a job in fashion—with a fashion magazine, let's say, or a store—your clothes become evidence of your imagination and your knowledge of the field. But even then, simplicity commands more respect than ostentation: classic styles, small patterns, dignified jewelry, subtle rather than dazzling colors. I might add that you needn't resort to decolletage or a dress that looks sprayed on. Interviewers will notice your figure even if you don't dress like a burlesque queen. Frankly, your chances of a job offer are better if the interviewer isn't worried that you'll be a distracting influence around the office.

What about those symbols of "artistic individuality": beards, walrus mustaches, waist-length pony tails, sandals, heavy black stockings, and other Greenwich Village trappings? Some interviewers are stuffy and resent such things, while others don't mind at all. If you've spent years cultivating a beard, a mustache, or flowing locks, these must mean a lot to you and I see no reason to chop them off. However, it won't hurt to *tame* the foliage a bit. Trim the beard and mustache regularly so you don't look like Robinson Crusoe. It does your pony tail no harm if you wear it in an elegant chignon. I'd leave sandals home if only because it's tiring to pound the pavement on such flimsy things. Besides, they don't go with a suit or dress. When it's too cold for nylons, an interviewer has no right to complain about black woolen stockings or tights.

What I'm really saying is that you have every right to be yourself. But do it with dignity, if only to avoid scaring off a good employer who's a bit square.

Planning the interview

Planning an interview really means deciding what you want a particular interviewer to know about you. What details of your education or experience will mean most to the employer you're going to visit tomorrow morning?

You plan an interview the same way you plan your job hunting letters. Your first step is to pin down one or two basic facts about the employer. Let's say tomorrow's appointment is with a commercial art studio This single fact tells you a great deal. Like most consulting firms, your potential employer is likely to have a variety of clients. This means that the office is probably interested in job hunters with *diversified* training and experience, plus what employers sometimes call a "client contact personality."

Your second step is to examine your background for details that prove you can fill this bill. It's not enough to recite your resume. The interviewer has already read it. Besides, the resume doesn't necessarily play up the particular details you want to emphasize in tomorrow's conversation. What are these details? If you're a beginner, you'll want to think back over the diverse school assignments that prove your flexibility. If you have some job experience, you'll want to examine your employment history for projects that demonstrate your versatility and "contact skills."

This doesn't mean you should stride into an interviewer's office with a prepared sales talk, like someone selling vacuum cleaners door to door. But you *should* have a mental outline of details that will appeal to your interviewer. He'll give you plenty of opportunity to talk about them. If not, you can steer the conversation in the right direction.

Once you're in the interviewer's office, watch the conversation for clues about facts that interest him. You can even pick up clues from the pictures on his walls. For example, architects often decorate their offices with photos of their new buildings. If one of these is a housing project and you've done some housing work, you have another sales point to bring up.

At times, you'll run across interviewers who give you no chance to steer the conversation in the right direction. Some interviewers will talk your ear off and barely allow you to speak. Others may say nothing, but just sit and wait for you to begin the conversation. All you can do is take the bull by the horns and say, "Though you have my resume, I think I should tell you a bit more about my background." The tongue-tied interviewer will be relieved that you've broken the silence in such a forthright way. Even the chatterbox may be pleased. He may jabber merely because he feels awkward, and he may be delighted when you take the initiative.

Showing and interpreting your portfolio

One of your main purposes in visiting an employer is to show him your portfolio. This will take a good part of the interview, perhaps most of it. In the previous chapter, "Planning Your Portfolio," I've talked about editing the portfolio to fit the interviewer. But you must also plan what you *say* about these samples. You must even plan your method of showing them.

If your portfolio is a looseleaf book or a stack of boards, showing your samples is simple. Just open your portfolio and let the interviewer thumb through *at his own pace*. Don't be surprised if he flips through your samples more quickly than you'd expected. This doesn't mean he's unimpressed. But he's probably seen hundreds of portfolios and learned to judge them in minutes. Before he's half way through your samples, he's sized you up. He'll look through the remaining samples just to confirm his first impression.

If you're using slides, showing your portfolio becomes trickier. In the previous chapter, I recommended a slide viewer rather than a projector. If you're using a hand fed model—not an automatic unit with a tray or cartridge of slides—you'd better rehearse the feeding operation. Is it best for *you* to insert the slides or should you let the interviewer put them in? It's considerate to give the interviewer his choice and have a few quick sentences ready to explain how the viewer works if *he* wants to run it. How should the slides be stacked? Should you mark them in one corner so you'll know where to grip them when you pick them up?

The toughest thing to plan is the commentary. You can't predict how fast the interviewer will turn pages or run through slides. How much should you say? I don't think you'll find it necessary to interpret *every* item. Many will explain *themselves* and you can remain silent. On the other hand, if you *do* have a significant point to make, try to keep your explanation down to one or two sentences: just as long as it takes for the interviewer to glance at the sample and move on. Don't make him pause politely while you launch into a lecture. If he wants more details, he'll ask.

How do you decide which samples need interpretation? There are two good reasons for adding explanatory comment. First, you should certainly explain if there's some essential point that the interviewer would never get if you didn't tell him. Let's say a color transparency was processed by a new, experimental method. Or perhaps a lush interior was done on an unusually low budget. The interviewer won't fully appreciate the sample unless you add this vital, but invisible detail.

The second reason brings us back to a question raised in the previous section: what do you want this interviewer to know about you? Does a sample embody some sales point that may ring the bell with this employer? Suppose you're applying for a job on the photographic staff of a magazine with a strong interest in science. You should certainly point out that a flower photo in your portfolio was part of a series on plant life. If you're showing graphic design samples to a book publisher, you may want to emphasize your schooling in book production. Wait till he turns to a page you set in the school's typographic shop and printed on a hand press. Then mention that you had a year's course in production.

You may feel that it's difficult to pack such information into one or two sentences. There's so much you *could* tell. But you must condense your message and take your chances on the interviewer asking for more facts. Don't be insulted if he just nods and doesn't pursue the subject. He's gotten your point.

This job of condensation takes planning. No need to memorize sentences or rehearse in front of a mirror. But go through your portfolio the day before the interview and decide what to say about each sample. Keep your running comments short, informal, like a one line caption under a magazine picture. "Built that model myself. It's life size. Stands about so high."

Questions you should be prepared to answer

Until now, I've concentrated on what *you'll* say. But you must also anticipate what your *interviewer* will say. A good interviewer asks questions, often embarrassing ones. You must be prepared for these. Here are some questions frequently asked by interviewers. Before your first interview, you should do some serious thinking about the answers you'll give.

(1) What was your school record?

If you're just out of school, this is a terribly important question. You have no job experience, except for a few summer jobs, perhaps, so your school record and portfolio are the interviewer's only evidence of your ability. Be prepared to give the interviewer a detailed account of your grades in various subjects. You needn't pull out a stack of report cards or school transcripts and read them aloud. It's simplest to talk in averages: "I averaged C in most foundation year subjects, but by the senior year I'd worked up to a B average in my major."

If your grades were poor, you must say so. But you may feel that your grades don't tell the real story. You may have good reasons: health problems, financial headaches, philosophical conflict with your teachers. If you have a valid explanation, be ready to present it.

(2) What have you done on the job?

Though your resume lists past employers and your duties on each job, the interviewer often wants more details. He may fire specific questions at you: "How was your department organized?" "What ideas did you contribute to this project?" Some interviewers prefer to ask general questions: "What do you think you learned from that job?" "Tell me more about your work." These broad questions may be a lazy interviewer's way of keeping up the conversation. But they may also be a sharp interviewer's way of saying. "The floor is yours. Tell me why I should hire you." This is the moment when your planning pays off. If you've examined your background for sales points that will appeal to this particular employer, you're well prepared.

Of course, not every question is an opportunity to raise a sales point. For some reason, the interviewer may want a particular fact, which you must be ready to supply. Before you step into someone's office, review your professional history carefully. Have you got all the names, dates, places, facts, and figures straight? You'd be amazed at the number of job hunters who can't recall bosses' names, projects, or dates of employment.

One effective way of marshalling your facts about a past job is to visualize a typical work day or work week. If an interviewer says, "Tell me more about that job," describing a typical day or week is a quick, logical way of covering a lot of territory.

(3) Why did you leave your last job?

There's nothing wrong with quitting because you're bored, underpaid, at odds with your boss, or stuck in a job with no future. Nor is there anything wrong with being laid off because business is bad or your department is being reorganized. You can speak frankly about these circumstances, though you should avoid *knocking* past employers, even if they deserve it. *Future* bosses often resent bitter words about *former* bosses.

But this becomes an awkward moment if you lost your job under unpleasant circumstances. What if you were fired because your boss was dissatisfied with your work? Many job hunters manage to conceal the reasons for losing a job. But a potential employer may respect you for telling the truth: "Yes, I was let go because the boss didn't like my work. But I'm confident that I *can* do good work. I was just in the wrong job." What seems like *bad* work in one office may be *good* work somewhere else. In an architectural office specializing in colonial houses, a designer who wants to do modern homes may be a total misfit. He becomes discouraged and his work may seem hopelessly inept. Put him to work in a different office and he may turn into a fireball.

What if you were fired for a really good reason? What do you tell an interviewer if you lost your job because of sloppy work, laziness, unwillingness to cooperate, or just plain bad manners?

Like many job hunters, you can try to hide the unpleasant facts. But keep in mind that a future boss will probably contact your past boss to get the facts. You may be *forced* to come clean. On the other hand, your personal code of honor may prompt you to tell the truth, *without* being forced. Again, you may be surprised at the number of bosses who'll respect your courage if you tell them frankly, "I turned in a rotten performance on my last job. But I've learned a lot from being fired. I won't make the same mistakes twice. I *can* turn in a first rate performance and I'd like another chance."

(4) What type of job are you looking for?

When an employer has a job to fill, he starts out with a mental picture of the man he wants. Sometimes this is a written *job description*, prepared by the personnel department. More often, it's a sketchy list of qualifications, tucked away in the interviewer's head. He also expects *you* to have some sort of job description in *your* head: some concept of the ideal spot for you. When the interviewer asks, "What type of job are you looking for?" he's really asking for some details of *your* job description to compare with his. If your concept of the right job seems close to his concept of the right man, he may offer you the job, provided your qualifications fill the bill. Of course, even if the two job descriptions don't match, he may be impressed and may want to hire you anyway.

You must have some specific ideas about the kind of job you hope to land. If you're a graphic designer, would you rather work in the fast moving world of advertising and magazines or the more staid world of book publishing? As a teacher, would you be interested in doing some administrative work in addition to conducting your classes?

But how do you answer an employer when he asks a question as vague as, "What sort of job do you want?" When you walk into a large organization, it obviously makes no sense to announce that you'd like to work in a small office. Nor is it honest to say that you'd like to work in a big place if you don't mean it. The logical way to state your position is to say: "I'd prefer a fairly intimate set-up, either a small organization or a close knit department in a large organization." This is the truth, but tailored to the interviewer and stated flexibly, so that you don't discourage an offer. The offer may be too good to turn down.

(5) How much money do you want?

When an interviewer asks about money, this doesn't necessarily mean he's about to offer you a job. He *might* make you an offer. But more likely, he wants a figure to compare with the income requirements of other candidates for the job, or possibly just a figure to keep in mind in case he has an opening in the future. Or he may just be curious.

Whatever his reasons for asking, you'd better have an answer ready, well in advance of the interview. In deciding your answer, you must consider several things:

First, how much money do you *need?* If you're single, living with your parents, you probably need less money than if you're married, with a couple of children. It's worthwhile to take a careful look at your living expenses and come up with a minimum figure, the lowest income you can accept without working nights or going into debt.

Second, find out the *going rate* for someone with your training and experience. Ask friends in the field what their offices would pay someone like you. The figure may vary from city to city, as well as from one organization to another. Your friends won't all come up with the same figure, but if you get enough figures they'll begin to form a pattern.

Third, you should certainly keep your previous earnings in mind, if you've already held a job. Unless your pay was far above or below the going rate, you can reasonably expect as much money in your *next* job, hopefully more.

Finally, you can use recent job offers—you may have *several* before you accept one—as an index of your current value in the talent market. Again, the figures will vary: one employer may be willing to pay more than another. But again you may find that the various offers form a pattern.

You can't feed all these figures into a computer and come up with the exact salary you can command. But by balancing these four factors, you can visualize a *potential salary range*. The bottom figure in this salary range is the minimum you think it's reasonable to accept. The top figure is the maximum you can ask without seeming *unreasonable*.

When the moment comes to name your salary requirements, I think there are two rules worth remembering. First, since most interviewers will ask about past earnings, be prepared to state these figures frankly. Second, give a good reason to justify the salary you're asking. Don't just say, "I'd like $7,000." It's far more persuasive to say, "I made $6,000 on my last job. My current offers average $7,000." To an interviewer, this indicates that you've come up with a realistic figure based on facts, not just on a hunch.

What if your last salary was unusually low? If you tell an interviewer what you earned, won't he use this as an excuse to offer you less than you deserve? I still think the most effective method is to lay your cards on the table: "I accepted a low salary on my last job because the job was a good opportunity to learn the ropes. But the going rate for someone with my experience is much higher now and I feel justified in asking $2,000 more."

Not all employers will ask you to name your price. Some will simply make you an offer. But your advance calculations are still useful when it's the employer, not you, who begins the bargaining by naming a figure. If his offer seems low, you have good reasons for naming a higher figure—and you can state these reasons frankly.

As you can see, salary negotiations are often like old fashioned horse trading. There may be lots of bargaining before you and the employer agree on the price. If your first asking price, or the employer's first offering price, seems fair to both of you, the negotiations may stop right there. You've made a deal. But if the two figures are far apart, one of you, or both, may have to yield a bit. If the employer wants you badly, he may raise the ante and meet your price. If the job is attractive enough, you may be willing to lower your price and accept the employer's offer. Or you may both give way and arrive at a compromise figure. Naturally, there are times when neither you nor the employer will budge. Your negotiations simply end at that point and your job hunt goes on.

(6) Who are your references?

In the chapter on writing your resume, I suggested that you leave out references. Instead, I recommended that you carry a variety of references in a pocket address book, so you can select names that will mean most to each employer. As I explained, there's no predicting what references an interviewer will want. Some prefer to contact your former bosses. Other interviewers may want the names of your teachers. Still others prefer so-called character references. Many ask for an assortment. It's wise to have a full list to choose from.

If you're just out of school, your teachers are important references. This also holds true if you've been out of school just a short time and you've had only one or two jobs. Which teachers will give you the best send-off? Naturally, you'll want to refer an employer to teachers who worked with you closely and gave you good grades. Selecting the right teachers is especially vital if your grades weren't uniformly good. Most students do good work in some subjects, but not in others. A teacher who saw you do good work in his class will be able to talk about your strong points. You can't expect him to *conceal* your weaker points. But having seen you at your best, he can explain your weaker points sympathetically.

Can your future employer contact *past* employers? If you left your past jobs on friendly terms, you won't hesitate to say: "Sure, my former bosses will tell you whatever you want to know." But what if you're not on friendly terms with an ex-boss? What if you're currently employed and you don't want your present boss to know that you're job hunting? In either case, you must explain the circumstances frankly to your potential employer. At the same time, you must suggest someone else who'll vouch for you. Can you count on a reference from a former co-worker who was fairly high on the ladder? Do you now have a high level co-worker who'll keep your secret and give you a good reference?

Whom can you turn to for a character reference? Are there respected members of the community who've known you and your family for many years? A good character reference needn't be an *obvious* pillar of the community, like your clergyman, a local political leader, or the president of the bank where you do business. An intelligent friend will do just as well.

In fact, a local clergyman, political figure or bank president may *not* be a good character reference unless he really knows you well. Don't ask a casual acquaintance for a letter of recommendation, just because he has an impressive title. Chances are that he'll write a cordial, but lukewarm letter that prompts the reader to say: "Oh, anybody can get a polite letter out of his State Assemblyman."

There are many other people who might provide valuable references: former clients; officers of professional associations in your field; editors and critics who've written about you; museum curators and private collectors who've bought your work; distinguished professionals who know and respect you.

How many references should you have in your address book? Few employers want more than three or four. But you'd better be armed with more than you need. If you tap all the sources I've mentioned, your list may easily reach ten or twelve. On the other hand, a beginner won't be criticized if his references include only a couple of teachers, a summer employer, and a respected friend of the family.

Be sure to let someone know when you plan to give his name as a reference. You might even send him a copy of your resume to give him a clear idea of your professional goals. This is more than courtesy. With some advance notice, your man can refresh his memory about your qualifications and be better prepared when your prospective boss inquires.

How useful is the traditional reference letter that an employer gives you when you leave a job? Most of these notes are practically form letters. They generally begin with the impersonal phrase, "To Whom It May Concern." Then they go on with cut and dried sentences like, "During the three years he was employed by us, this employee fulfilled his duties in a satisfactory manner." There's no harm in showing these to a future employer, but they don't really tell him much. Unless these letters are unusually warm and detailed, your prospective boss must still contact previous employers for the vital facts.

Questions you will want to ask

Until now, we've assumed that the *interviewer* will ask the questions. But if you're offered a job, there are questions *you'll* want to ask before saying yes. Don't be shy about quizzing your future employer. He doesn't expect you to walk into a job with your eyes closed. He'll expect questions and he'll give you straight answers. If he doesn't,. think twice before you accept his offer.

Here are some questions to clarify before you take any job:

(1) *Are there other financial benefits beside salary?* Your salary may not be your only income from a job. There may be a profit sharing plan, annual bonuses, incentives for bringing in business, expense accounts, or overtime pay. Many employers have life, medical, and retirement insurance plans. They may divide the cost with you or foot the whole bill. This can add up to a lot of money over the years.

(2) *What are working hours, vacations, and holidays?* Some organizations work 9-to-5. Others stretch the day to 5:30 or 6. Still others work 8-to-4. These details can be important if you're commuting or going to school at night. It's also worthwhile to ask how much overtime is normal. Do you get paid for it or take equivalent time off? Some employers are more liberal than others about vacations and holidays. Though the normal summer vacation in a profit making organization is two weeks for a new employee, some employers give you three or four weeks after a number of years.

(3) *What's the organizational set-up?* What are the various departments? Who works for whom and who does what? Who's your immediate superior and can you meet him, if you haven't already? Are there other offices in other locations, or is this the only one? What do the other offices do? It's important to get some sense of the organization's scope and structure and just where you fit into the total picture.

(4) *What will be the nature of your work?* What sort of projects will you work on? If there are clients, who are they? How much initiative will you be given? What skills will you be expected to use? Will you have to travel? Where and how often? Can you see your future surroundings and the equipment you'll work with? Are you being hired for the duration of a specific project? For a limited probationary period? Or can you consider this a permanent job unless, of course, you don't pan out?

(5) *What are your prospects of advancement?* This is a tough question for an employer to answer, but you must try to find out if this is a dead end job or a job with a future. The employer can't make you any promises the moment you're hired, but he *can* say: "We have salary reviews every six months. We try to give raises when they're deserved. And we usually fill our high level jobs from our own ranks instead of bringing in an outsider." Or he might say: "This is a growing organization and a good man moves up as soon as he proves he can take more responsibility." Neither statement guarantees you anything. It's too early. But both statements promise you the chance to rise when you prove your value. That's as much as you can expect. I might add that a job "with no future," but with an interesting *present,* can still be worth taking for a year or two if the experience is valuable for your professional advancement in later jobs.

Circumstances may suggest other questions. If you must relocate from one city to another, you have a right to ask whether your new employer will pay the moving bill. If you've landed the job through an employment agency, you might ask tactfully whether there's any chance that the employer will pay your agency fee or split it with you. Many organizations absorb these expenses.

Follow-up letters

Most interviews *don't* end with a job offer. However, if you've made an impression, the interviewer will do his best to remember you. When a suitable job turns up, you may hear from him again.

You can help him remember you. Many personnel experts recommend that you drop a brief thank you note to everyone who interviews you. This is a sound idea if you don't make a big, time consuming campaign of it. A few minutes at the typewriter are all you need to bang out a brief, informal message:

"Just a brief note of thanks for your time and interest when we met on Monday afternoon. I enjoyed talking with you and I appreciate your constructive suggestions about my portfolio."

That's all you need. This note won't win you a job, but this extra bit of courtesy will leave its small mark.

Someone else who deserves a note is the man who told you: "Call Sam Parker and mention my name. He might know of a job for you." When you've seen Sam Parker, you owe a thank you note to the man who steered you to him. This is more than just a courteous gesture. Your note serves as a reminder that you're still job hunting. You might get a second steer from the same source, a steer you might not get without that note.

A third type of follow-up note might be written *after* you land a job. This is the time to review the names of all the interviewers who showed more than a casual interest: those who said, "I wish I had a job to offer you;" those who were generous with their time and advice; those who sent you to their friends. This may turn out to be quite a long list. But I think it's worth a few evenings of letter writing to tell these people:

"Remembering your generous interest in my job hunt, I

thought you might be pleased to learn that I've landed an excellent position. I'm now assistant to the Design Director of the Kenney Furniture Company. Again, my warmest thanks for your encouragement."

Just three sentences. But enough to reinforce a favorable impression. You're not looking for a job any longer, but some day you may be job hunting again. When that day comes, you'll hope that people remember you from your last job hunt.

This suggests an important tip: hold on to the stack of index cards on which you've kept track of your contacts. Many of these names will be useful throughout your professional life.

The job offer

If you've conducted your job hunt intelligently, you'll soon face the decisive moment. You'll be offered a job and you must say yes or no. If this is definitely the job you want, all you have to say is, "Fine! When do I start?"

But what if you have two conflicting job offers? You may not be prepared to decide between them on the spur of the moment. In this situation, you have every right to ask both employers: "May I have some time to think about your offer and discuss it with my family and friends?" If an employer is in a hurry, he may ask for an answer the following day. If he's less rushed, he may say, "Okay, how much time do you need?"

As always, I think you'll find it best to lay your cards on the table. What if Employer A offers you more money, but Employer B offers you a more exciting job? I think it's fair to go to Employer B and say: "I'd like to work for you, but frankly I'm in a spot. Another organization has offered me more money. With a wife and kids, I have no right to turn down a higher paycheck. Would you be willing to reconsider your salary figure?" No responsible employer will blame you for telling him the truth. He'll probably be just as straightforward. He may ask you frankly, "How much is your other offer?" He'll then tell you whether he can match it or at least make a compromise offer.

Another complication may be the job offer that isn't *quite* an offer. The employer may say: "We're going to make our decision at a meeting Friday morning. If you have any other offers pending, can you put off your decision until Friday?" This is a reasonable request. If you *can* wait until Friday for his decision, you should certainly agree, with the promise that you'll phone if you get a conflicting offer that demands a decision *before* Friday. If you can't wait till Friday—perhaps another employer wants you to say yes or no tomorrow—say so. It's possible that the Friday meeting can be scheduled earlier, if you're wanted badly enough.

But at last the right offer comes and you accept. Your new boss says, "Congratulations! You start three weeks from Monday." Usually, these words and a handshake consummate the bargain. Except for teachers and some top executives, few artists, designers, or architects get an actual contract. However, many employers make things official by sending you a confirming note stating salary, starting date, department, and your title, if you have one. If you receive no confirming note, I suggest that *you* send one, just for the record:

"Thanks again for your confidence in me. As we agree, I'll report for work in the package design department on Monday morning, November 7. I understand that my salary will be $400 a month and that I'm on a six month probationary period, at the end of which we'll review my work and salary. I look forward to joining you."

This brief letter summarizes the verbal agreement. The second sentence tactfully mentions a promise made by the employer. No one would call this letter a contract. But it puts the facts on record and it's morally, if not legally, binding.

Your job hunt is ended. On that Monday morning, a new phase in your life begins. Now no book can help you. Your fate is in your own hands.

Part Four
Schools and
Professional Organizations

19
Directory of
degree granting schools

What are the nation's major art schools, college and university art departments? What are the most important schools in your state and the states nearby? What subjects do they teach? Which schools are for men only? Which are for women only? Which ones are co-educational? Which schools may provide scholarships, fellowships or other financial aid if you can't meet all the expenses of your professional training?

The charts in this directory are meant to answer these basic questions, the first questions you'll ask when you begin the difficult job of choosing a school.

How was the list compiled?

All colleges and universities and *nearly* all leading art schools grant degrees. To most art educators and employers, the degree is a symbol (though certainly not a guarantee) of thorough professional training and a rich cultural background. Therefore, it seems reasonable to limit the list to degree granting schools.

Since this is a directory of *major* schools, the list is restricted to schools that grant a substantial number of degrees each year. For this information, I've relied on the latest edition of *Earned Degrees Conferred*, published by the Office of Education of the United States Department of Health, Education and Welfare. In theory, each school on my list granted at least ten degrees in *one* of the following areas: architecture, art education, fine art or applied art. In reality, a *few* outstanding schools fell slightly short of the ten degree minimum. Nevertheless, these *do* appear in the directory.

Course lists and other data in the directory come from the schools themselves: the facts are based on a series of questionnaire surveys made by the author and the editors of the magazine, *American Artist.*

Excluded from the directory are: (a) schools that grant no degrees, (b) schools that grant too few degrees, (c) junior colleges, (d) correspondence schools, (e) private classes conducted by an artist in his own studio, (f) community centers, YMCAs, YMHAs and adult education schools, (g) schools that operate only in the summer, (h) and schools that grant degrees only in art history, with no studio courses required.

Also excluded are schools that failed to return questionnaires, despite repeated reminders, and schools that returned questionnaires so vague or incomplete that the material was useless. In some cases, I was able to find missing facts in the American Federation of Arts' *American Art Directory.* But in other cases, I was forced to give up and simply publish an incomplete listing or exclude a school altogether, for lack of information.

How to use this list

The fact that a school appears on the list is no guarantee that the school is good. This is just a list of the schools that grant enough degrees to *suggest* that the institution offers an art program of reasonable size. Before you pick a school, you must still write for catalogs, talk to your high school teachers and guidance counselors, interview alumni, and visit the schools themselves. No directory can answer the fourteen vital questions listed in Chapter 4 on "Choosing an Art School." You must find the answers yourself.

Nor can you assume that the schools in this directory are the *only* ones worth considering. There may be lesser known schools in your neighborhood which are as good. This may be particularly true in the fine art fields—painting, sculpture, and printmaking—which may be taught equally well on a large university campus or in one man's attic studio.

In short, some *good* schools may be left out and some *bad* schools may be included. Furthermore, there's also a certain percentage of incomplete or inaccurate data, simply because someone wouldn't take the trouble to fill out a questionnaire carefully. And keep in mind that school programs often change: some of these listings may be out of date in a matter of months.

Like any school directory, this list must be read with an awareness of its limitations. This directory does nothing more than suggest *some* of the schools you should investigate. Your investigations may lead you to choose one of these schools or to reject the whole pack and pick one that's not on the list. The directory may actually help you choose an *unlisted* school. When you've investigated several well known schools on the list, you'll be better equipped to judge little known schools that may turn out to be just as good.

Accreditation

Only two professional associations in the art field issue a list of accredited schools. The approval of the National Association of Schools of Art is indicated by the code letter A in the column labeled "Accreditation." The National Architectural Accrediting Board has puts its stamp of approval on a few dozen schools, all of which appear on my list. The code letter N signifies this in the column labeled "Accreditation." Needless to say, not all schools accredited by the National Architectural Accrediting Board or the National Association of Schools of Art are equally good; but the approval of these two groups indicates that a school meets certain *basic* standards, at least.

Notes on the charts

Here are a few notes that may help you as you read the charts on the following pages.

Schools are listed by state. The states are in alphabetical order and the schools are in alphabetical order within each state. Each school's name is followed by the city where the school is located.

Degrees are often granted jointly by two institutions. An art school may arrange for its students to attend a nearby college or university for courses in the liberal arts and the sciences. Conversely, a college or university may send students to a nearby art school for studio courses. Your degree may be granted by the art school *or* by the college or university.

Subjects listed may be majors, areas of concentration, minors, or simply courses that form part of a general art major. In a large university, consisting of many different schools, these subjects may be taught in several divisions and departments. For example, architecture is sometimes part of a university's school of agriculture or engineering. Interior design, oddly enough, is often taught in the school of home economics. Fabric design is a common subject in a school of education. Read university catalogs carefully to find out *how many* classes are given in a subject and *where* they're taught.

Architecture may include separate curricula in landscape architecture and city planning. If a school isn't marked N, signifying accreditation by the National Architectural Accrediting Board, the program may actually be pre-architecture. Such courses prepare the student for later enrollment in the professional program of an accredited architectural school.

Art teaching most often means preparation for elementary or secondary school teaching. An art education program frequently includes one or two courses in each subject listed on the chart. This doesn't mean that the teacher receives *professional* training in each of these fields. In most cases, these are merely introductory courses.

Fabric design may mean printed fabrics, weaving, fabric technology, or a blend of all three.

Graphic design may mean a complete program in the design of all types of printed matter or it may mean specialized subjects like book design, advertising design, or packaging.

Illustration may be a general course or it may mean a specialty like fashion drawing or technical illustration.

Commercial art is a term used by many schools for a program that combines graphic design and illustration. When I have found this term on a school's questionnaire, I have listed *both* subjects on the chart.

Industrial design may emphasize a specialty like automotive design or packaging, or it may cover the entire field.

Interior design may be a general program, or it may concentrate on a specialty like commercial interiors or furniture design.

Photography may be still or motion pictures. The latter may be part of a program in motion picture production.

Painting, sculpture, and printmaking all imply drawing. A school rarely, if ever, offers drawing as a major, so the chart contains no separate category for the subject. Printmaking may mean a broad program in many techniques, or just one or two processes, like etching or lithography.

Men and women may both be admitted to a university, but they may actually attend separate schools within the university. Read catalogs carefully to see which schools are really co-educational.

Scholarships is a general term I've used to cover all types of financial aid. The more common types of financial assistance include full tuition scholarships, graduate fellowships, and student loans. Keep in mind that the scope of financial aid varies enormously. Some schools can afford nothing more than half-tuition scholarships, while others may be able to cover the student's entire tuition and living expenses.

The charts don't necessarily list a school's complete program. Many teach other subjects and even offer other majors in the art field. The subjects listed on the charts simply correspond to the fields described in *Art Career Guide*.

	Accreditation	Architecture	Art Teaching	Fabric Design	Graphic Design	Illustration	Industrial Design	Interior Design	Painting	Photography	Printmaking	Sculpture	Men	Women	Scholarships
ALABAMA															
Alabama College, Montevallo			•	•	•			•	•		•	•	•	•	•
Auburn University, Auburn	AN	•	•		•	•	•	•	•		•	•	•	•	•
Troy State College, Troy			•		•				•	•		•	•	•	•
University of Alabama, University			•		•	•			•		•	•	•	•	•
ARIZONA															
Arizona State University, Tempe	N	•	•		•	•		•	•	•	•	•	•	•	•
University of Arizona, Tucson	N	•	•	•	•	•			•		•	•	•	•	•
ARKANSAS															
Arkansas Polytechnic Coll., Russellville		•	•	•	•	•	•		•		•		•	•	•
University of Arkansas, Fayetteville	N	•	•		•	•	•	•	•		•	•	•	•	•
CALIFORNIA															
Art Center Coll. of Design, Los Angeles	A				•	•	•	•	•	•			•	•	•
Cal. Coll. of Arts & Crafts, Oakland	A	•	•	•	•	•	•	•	•	•	•	•	•	•	•
Cal. St. Polytechnic Coll., S. L. Obispo	N	•											•	•	
Chico State College, Chico			•	•	•				•		•	•	•	•	•
Chouinard Art Inst., Los Angeles	A		•		•	•	•	•	•			•	•	•	•
Claremont Graduate School, Claremont				•	•	•	•	•	•		•	•	•	•	•
Dominican College, San Rafael			•									•			
Fresno State College, Fresno			•	•	•	•			•	•	•	•	•	•	•
Heald Engineering Coll., San Francisco		•										•			
Long Beach State Coll., Long Beach			•	•	•	•	•	•	•		•	•	•	•	•
Los Angeles State Coll., Los Angeles									•				•	•	•
Mills College, Oakland			•						•	•	•	•		•	•
Otis Art Institute, Los Angeles						•			•		•	•	•	•	•
Sacramento State College, Sacramento			•		•	•			•	•	•	•	•	•	•
San Diego State College, San Diego			•		•		•	•	•		•	•	•	•	•
San Fernando Valley St.Coll.,Northridge			•						•	•	•	•	•	•	•
San Francisco Art Inst. Coll., S. Fran.	A		•		•	•			•	•	•	•	•	•	•
San Francisco State Coll., San Francisco			•	•	•			•	•	•	•	•	•	•	•
San Jose State College, San Jose			•	•	•	•		•	•		•	•	•	•	•
Scripps College, Claremont			•	•					•		•	•		•	•
Stanford University, Stanford		•	•						•				•	•	•
University of California, Berkeley	N	•	•	•				•	•		•	•	•	•	•
University of California, Davis			•			•			•		•	•	•	•	•
University of California, Los Angeles			•		•	•	•	•	•	•	•	•	•	•	•
University of California, Santa Barbara			•						•	•	•	•	•	•	•
University of So. Cal., Los Angeles	N	•	•		•			•	•		•	•	•	•	•
Woodbury College, Los Angeles			•		•	•		•					•	•	

	Accreditation	Architecture	Art Teaching	Fabric Design	Graphic Design	Illustration	Industrial Design	Interior Design	Painting	Photography	Printmaking	Sculpture	Men	Women	Scholarships
COLORADO															
Colorado College, Colorado Springs			•						•		•	•	•	•	•
Colorado State College, Greeley			•	•	•	•			•	•	•	•	•	•	•
Colorado State University, Ft. Collins			•	•	•	•		•	•		•	•	•	•	•
University of Colorado, Boulder	N	•							•	•	•	•	•	•	•
University of Denver, Denver			•	•	•	•		•	•		•	•	•	•	•
Western State Coll. of Colo., Gunnison			•		•				•		•	•	•	•	
CONNECTICUT															
Connecticut College, New London						•			•		•	•		•	
Southern Conn. State Coll., New Haven		•							•		•	•	•	•	•
University of Bridgeport, Bridgeport		•			•	•			•		•	•	•	•	•
University of Hartford, Hartford	A	•			•				•		•	•	•	•	
Yale University, New Haven	N	•			•	•			•	•	•	•	•		•
DELAWARE															
University of Delaware, Newark			•	•		•		•	•		•	•	•	•	•
DISTRICT OF COLUMBIA															
American University			•		•		•	•	•		•	•	•	•	•
Catholic University of America	N	•	•		•				•		•	•	•	•	•
Corcoran School of Art					•	•			•		•	•	•	•	•
George Washington University			•		•	•			•			•	•	•	•
Howard University	N	•	•		•	•			•		•			•	•
FLORIDA															
Florida State University, Tallahassee			•	•	•	•	•		•		•	•	•	•	•
University of Florida, Gainesville	N	•	•			•			•	•	•	•	•	•	•
University of Miami, Coral Gables		•	•		•	•	•	•	•		•	•	•		•
GEORGIA															
Georgia Inst. of Tech., Atlanta	N	•				•							•	•	
University of Georgia, Athens		•	•	•	•	•	•	•	•	•	•	•	•	•	•
HAWAII															
University of Hawaii, Honolulu			•	•	•				•		•	•	•	•	
IDAHO															
University of Idaho, Moscow		•		•	•	•			•		•	•	•	•	

	Accreditation	Architecture	Art Teaching	Fabric Design	Graphic Design	Illustration	Industrial Design	Interior Design	Painting	Photography	Printmaking	Sculpture	Men	Women	Scholarships
ILLINOIS															
Art Institute of Chicago, Chicago	A		•	•	•	•	•	•	•	•	•	•	•	•	•
Bradley University, Peoria			•	•	•	•			•		•	•	•	•	•
Illinois Inst., of Tech., Chicago	AN	•	•			•	•	•		•	•	•	•	•	•
Illinois State Univ., Normal			•						•		•	•	•	•	•
Illinois Wesleyan Univ., Bloomington			•	•	•		•	•	•	•	•	•	•	•	•
Northern Illinois Univ., De Kalb			•	•	•	•	•	•	•	•	•	•	•	•	•
Northwestern University, Evanston			•			•			•	•		•	•	•	•
So. Illinois University, Carbondale		•	•	•	•	•	•	•	•	•	•	•	•	•	•
University of Chicago, Chicago			•						•		•	•	•	•	•
University of Illinois, Urbana	AN	•	•	•	•	•	•		•	•	•	•	•	•	•
INDIANA															
Ball State Teachers College, Muncie			•	•	•		•	•	•	•	•	•	•	•	•
De Pauw University, Greencastle		•	•	•	•	•	•	•	•	•	•	•	•	•	•
Indiana State University, Terre Haute			•		•			•	•		•	•	•	•	•
Indiana University, Bloomington			•	•	•	•	•	•	•	•	•	•	•	•	•
John Herron Art Inst., Indianapolis	N		•		•	•			•		•	•	•	•	•
Purdue University, Lafayette			•		•	•	•	•	•	•	•	•	•	•	•
St. Mary's College, Notre Dame			•	•	•	•			•	•	•	•		•	•
Univ. of Notre Dame, Notre Dame	N	•	•				•		•		•	•	•		•
IOWA															
Clarke College, Dubuque			•	•	•		•	•			•	•		•	•
Drake University, Des Moines			•	•	•	•		•	•			•	•	•	•
Iowa State College, Cedar Falls			•	•	•	•			•			•	•	•	•
Iowa State University, Ames	N	•							•				•	•	•
University of Iowa, Iowa City		•	•	•	•	•	•	•	•	•	•	•	•	•	•
KANSAS															
Fort Hays Kansas State Coll., Hays			•		•	•			•	•	•	•	•	•	•
Kansas State Teachers Coll., Emporia			•		•	•			•	•	•	•	•	•	•
Kansas State Coll., Pittsburg			•			•	•		•		•	•	•	•	•
Kansas State University, Manhattan	N	•	•		•	•	•	•	•		•	•	•	•	•
University of Kansas, Lawrence	N	•	•	•	•	•	•	•	•		•	•	•	•	•
University of Wichita, Wichita			•		•	•			•		•	•	•	•	•
KENTUCKY															
Eastern Kentucky State Coll., Richmond			•						•		•	•	•	•	
Murray State University, Murray			•	•	•	•			•	•	•	•	•	•	•
University of Kentucky, Lexington	N	•	•						•	•	•	•	•	•	•

LOUISIANA

School	Accreditation	Architecture	Art Teaching	Fabric Design	Graphic Design	Illustration	Industrial Design	Interior Design	Painting	Photography	Printmaking	Sculpture	Men	Women	Scholarships
Louisiana State Univ., Baton Rouge	N	•	•		•			•	•		•	•	•	•	•
Tulane University, New Orleans	N	•	•						•		•	•	•	•	•

MARYLAND

School	Accreditation	Architecture	Art Teaching	Fabric Design	Graphic Design	Illustration	Industrial Design	Interior Design	Painting	Photography	Printmaking	Sculpture	Men	Women	Scholarships
Maryland Institute, Baltimore	A	•	•	•	•	•	•	•	•	•	•	•	•	•	•
University of Maryland, College Park		•	•			•			•		•	•	•	•	•

MASSACHUSETTS

School	Accreditation	Architecture	Art Teaching	Fabric Design	Graphic Design	Illustration	Industrial Design	Interior Design	Painting	Photography	Printmaking	Sculpture	Men	Women	Scholarships
Boston Museum School, Boston	A		•		•	•		•	•	•	•	•	•	•	•
Boston University, Boston			•		•	•		•	•	•	•	•	•	•	•
Brandeis University, Waltham			•	•	•	•	•	•	•				•	•	•
Harvard Univ., Cambridge (incl. Radcliffe Coll.)	N	•							•				•	•	•
Massachusetts College of Art, Boston	A	•	•	•	•	•	•		•	•	•	•	•	•	•
Mass. Inst. of Tech., Cambridge	N	•											•	•	•
Mt. Holyoke College, South Hadley									•		•	•		•	•
Smith College, Northampton			•						•		•	•		•	•
S.E. Mass. Tech. Inst., Fall River				•	•	•			•	•	•			•	•
Tufts University, Medford		•	•	•	•	•	•	•	•	•	•	•	•	•	•
University of Massachusetts, Amherst		•	•						•		•	•	•	•	•
Wellesley College, Wellesley			•				•		•			•		•	•
Wheaton College, Norton									•	•				•	•
Williams College, Williamstown		•					•		•		•	•	•		•
Worcester Art Mus. Sch., Worcester	A	•			•				•		•	•	•	•	•

MICHIGAN

School	Accreditation	Architecture	Art Teaching	Fabric Design	Graphic Design	Illustration	Industrial Design	Interior Design	Painting	Photography	Printmaking	Sculpture	Men	Women	Scholarships
Central Michigan Univ., Mt. Pleasant			•	•					•		•	•	•	•	•
Cranbrook Acad. of Art, Bloomfield Hills	A	•	•	•					•		•	•	•	•	•
Eastern Michigan Univ., Ypsilanti			•						•		•	•	•	•	•
Michigan State Univ., East Lansing		•	•		•			•	•		•	•	•	•	•
Northern Michigan Univ., Marquette			•	•	•	•	•	•	•	•	•	•	•	•	•
University of Detroit, Detroit	N	•			•	•			•		•	•	•	•	•
University of Michigan, Ann Arbor	AN	•	•		•	•	•	•	•		•	•	•	•	•
Wayne State University, Detroit			•	•	•	•	•	•	•		•	•	•	•	•
Western Michigan Univ., Kalamazoo			•	•	•				•		•	•	•	•	•

MINNESOTA

School	Accreditation	Architecture	Art Teaching	Fabric Design	Graphic Design	Illustration	Industrial Design	Interior Design	Painting	Photography	Printmaking	Sculpture	Men	Women	Scholarships
Mankato State College, Mankato			•	•					•		•	•	•	•	•
Minneapolis Sch. of Art, Minneapolis	A				•	•	•		•		•	•	•	•	•
University of Minnesota, Duluth			•						•		•	•	•	•	•
University of Minnesota, Minneapolis	N	•	•						•	•	•	•	•	•	•

	Accreditation	Architecture	Art Teaching	Fabric Design	Graphic Design	Illustration	Industrial Design	Interior Design	Painting	Photography	Printmaking	Sculpture	Men	Women	Scholarships
MISSISSIPPI															
Miss. State Coll. for Women, Columbus			•		•	•		•	•		•	•		•	
University of Mississippi, University			•		•			•	•		•	•	•	•	
MISSOURI															
Kansas City Art Inst., Kansas City	A				•	•	•	•	•	•	•	•	•	•	•
Northeast Missouri State Teachers Coll., Kirksville			•		•				•		•		•	•	
Notre Dame College, St. Louis			•						•		•	•			
S. E. Mo. State Coll., Cape Girardeau			•	•	•	•			•		•	•	•	•	•
University of Missouri, Columbia		•	•						•		•	•	•	•	•
University of Missouri, Kansas City					•				•			•	•	•	•
Washington Univ., St. Louis	AN	•	•		•	•			•		•	•	•	•	•
MONTANA															
Montana State University, Bozeman	N		•		•		•	•	•		•	•	•	•	
NEBRASKA															
University of Nebraska, Lincoln	N	•	•		•	•			•		•	•	•	•	
NEW HAMPSHIRE															
Dartmouth College, Hanover		•							•	•	•	•			•
University of New Hampshire, Durham			•			•			•	•	•	•	•	•	•
NEW JERSEY															
Coll. of St. Elizabeth, Convent Station			•					•	•		•	•		•	
Glassboro State Coll., Glassboro			•					•	•		•	•	•	•	
Jersey City State Coll., Jersey City			•	•	•				•		•		•	•	
Montclair State College, Montclair			•	•				•	•	•	•	•	•	•	•
Newark State College, Newark			•	•	•		•		•	•	•	•	•	•	•
Paterson State College, Paterson			•										•	•	•
Princeton University, Princeton	N	•							•				•		•
Rutgers State University, Rutgers			•						•		•	•	•	•	•
NEW MEXICO															
University of N. Mexico, Albuquerque			•						•	•	•	•	•	•	•

	Accreditation	Architecture	Art Teaching	Fabric Design	Graphic Design	Illustration	Industrial Design	Interior Design	Painting	Photography	Printmaking	Sculpture	Men	Women	Scholarships
NEW YORK															
Adelphi College, Garden City			•		•	•		•	•		•	•	•	•	•
Alfred University, Alfred	A				•				•	•	•	•	•	•	•
Brooklyn College, Brooklyn		•	•	•	•			•	•	•	•	•	•	•	•
City College, New York			•						•		•	•	•	•	•
College of New Rochelle, New Rochelle			•	•	•	•	•	•	•	•	•			•	•
Columbia University, New York	N	•	•	•				•	•	•	•	•	•	•	•
Cooper Union, New York	AN	•			•	•			•	•	•	•	•	•	•
Cornell University, Ithaca	N	•	•	•	•	•	•	•	•		•	•	•	•	•
Hofstra University, Hempstead			•	•	•				•		•	•	•	•	•
Hunter College, New York			•						•		•	•	•	•	•
Ithaca College, Ithaca									•	•		•	•	•	
Marymount College, Tarrytown			•		•	•	•		•		•	•		•	•
New York University, New York			•	•	•	•			•	•	•	•	•	•	•
Parsons School of Design, New York	A				•	•	•	•	•		•		•	•	•
Pratt Institute, Brooklyn	AN	•	•		•	•	•	•	•	•	•	•	•	•	•
Queens College, Flushing			•	•	•			•	•		•	•	•	•	•
Rensselaer Polytechnic Inst., Troy	N	•											•	•	•
Rochester Inst. of Tech., Rochester		•	•	•	•	•	•	•	•	•	•	•	•	•	•
Rosary Hill College, Buffalo			•					•	•	•	•	•		•	•
Skidmore College, Skidmore			•	•	•	•			•	•	•	•		•	
State Univ. College, Buffalo			•	•	•			•	•	•	•	•	•	•	•
State Univ. College, New Paltz			•		•			•	•	•	•	•	•	•	•
State Univ. Coll. of Forestry, Syracuse		•											•	•	•
State Univ. of New York, Buffalo	A	•	•						•	•	•	•	•	•	•
Syracuse University, Syracuse	AN	•	•	•	•	•	•	•	•	•	•	•	•	•	•
Vassar College, Poughkeepsie		•	•		•	•		•	•			•		•	•
NORTH CAROLINA															
East Carolina College, Greenville	A		•	•	•	•	•	•	•		•	•	•	•	
North Carolina State Univ., Raleigh	N	•						•	•	•	•	•	•	•	
University of N. Carolina, Chapel Hill			•						•		•	•	•	•	•
Women's Coll., Univ. of N. Carolina, Greensboro			•	•	•	•	•	•	•		•	•		•	•
NORTH DAKOTA															
No. Dakota State Univ., Fargo		•											•	•	•

	Accreditation	Architecture	Art Teaching	Fabric Design	Graphic Design	Illustration	Industrial Design	Interior Design	Painting	Photography	Printmaking	Sculpture	Men	Women	Scholarships
OHIO															
Antioch College, Yellow Springs			•						•			•	•	•	•
Art Academy, Cincinnati	A				•	•			•		•	•	•	•	•
Bowling Green St. Univ., Bowling Green			•						•		•	•	•	•	•
Cleveland Inst. of Art, Cleveland	A		•	•	•	•	•	•	•		•	•	•	•	•
Dayton Art Inst., Dayton	A				•	•	•		•		•	•	•	•	
Kent State University, Kent	N	•	•		•		•		•				•	•	•
Miami University, Oxford	N	•	•	•	•	•			•		•	•	•	•	•
Oberlin College, Oberlin		•	•						•			•	•	•	•
Ohio State Univ., Columbus	N	•	•		•	•	•	•	•	•	•	•	•	•	•
Ohio University, Athens	N	•	•	•	•	•	•	•	•	•	•	•	•	•	•
Ohio Wesleyan Univ., Delaware			•						•			•	•	•	•
Univ. of Cincinnati, Cincinnati	AN	•	•		•	•	•	•	•	•	•	•	•	•	•
Western Reserve Univ., Cleveland	N	•	•	•	•	•	•	•	•			•	•	•	•
Wittenberg University, Springfield			•	•	•	•	•	•	•		•	•	•	•	•
Youngstown University, Youngstown			•										•	•	•
OKLAHOMA															
Central State College, Edmond			•		•				•		•	•	•	•	•
Oklahoma State Univ., Stillwater	N	•			•				•		•		•	•	
Univ. of Oklahoma, Norman	N	•	•		•	•	•		•		•	•	•	•	•
Univ. of Tulsa, Tulsa			•		•	•			•		•	•	•	•	•
OREGON															
Portland Museum Art Sch., Portland	A				•	•			•		•	•	•	•	•
Univ. of Oregon, Eugene	N	•	•	•		•		•	•			•	•	•	•
PENNSYLVANIA															
Carnegie Inst. of Tech., Pittsburgh	AN	•	•	•	•	•	•		•	•	•	•	•	•	•
Edinboro State College, Edinboro			•		•				•		•	•	•	•	•
Indiana Univ. of Pennsylvania, Indiana			•						•		•	•	•	•	•
Kutztown State College, Kutztown			•	•		•	•	•	•	•	•	•	•	•	•
Moore College of Art, Philadelphia	A		•	•	•	•		•	•	•	•			•	•
Pa. Acad. of Fine Arts, Philadelphia						•			•		•	•	•	•	•
Pa. State Univ., University Park	N	•	•	•	•	•		•	•	•	•	•	•	•	•
Philadelphia Coll. of Art, Philadelphia	A		•	•	•	•	•	•	•	•	•	•		•	•
Swarthmore College, Swarthmore									•		•	•	•	•	•
Temple University, Philadelphia	A		•	•	•	•			•		•	•	•	•	•
Univ. of Pennsylvania, Philadelphia	N	•	•					•	•		•	•		•	•
Wilson College, Chambersburg									•		•	•		•	•

	Accreditation	Architecture	Art Teaching	Fabric Design	Graphic Design	Illustration	Industrial Design	Interior Design	Painting	Photography	Printmaking	Sculpture	Men	Women	Scholarships
RHODE ISLAND															
Brown University, Providence									•		•	•	•	•	•
R. I. School of Design, Providence	AN	•	•	•	•	•	•	•	•	•	•	•	•	•	•
SOUTH CAROLINA															
Bob Jones University, Greenville			•		•	•			•		•	•	•	•	
Clemson University, Clemson	N	•											•	•	•
Univ. of South Carolina, Columbia			•		•			•	•		•	•	•	•	•
TENNESSEE															
Geo. Peabody Coll. for Teachers, Nashville			•	•					•		•	•	•		
Memphis Academy of Arts, Memphis	A		•	•	•			•	•		•	•	•	•	•
Memphis State Univ., Memphis			•		•	•		•	•		•	•	•	•	
TEXAS															
North Texas State Univ., Denton		•	•	•	•	•		•	•		•		•	•	•
Rice University, Houston	N	•							•		•	•	•	•	•
Sam Houston State Teachers Coll., Huntsville			•		•	•			•		•	•	•	•	
Southern Methodist Univ., Dallas			•		•	•	•	•	•		•	•	•	•	•
Texas A & M Univ., College Station	N	•										•			
Texas Christian Univ., Ft. Worth			•		•	•				•	•		•	•	
Texas Tech. College, Lubbock	N	•	•		•	•	•	•	•		•		•	•	•
Texas Women's Univ., Denton			•	•	•	•		•	•	•	•	•		•	•
Univ. of Houston, Houston	N	•	•		•	•	•	•	•	•	•	•	•	•	•
Univ. of Texas, Austin	N	•	•	•	•	•		•	•	•	•	•	•	•	•
West Texas State Univ., Canyon			•	•	•				•		•	•	•	•	•
UTAH															
Brigham Young Univ., Provo			•					•	•		•	•	•	•	•
Univ. of Utah, Salt Lake City	N	•	•		•	•	•		•		•	•	•	•	•
Utah State Univ., Logan			•										•	•	•
VERMONT															
Bennington College, Bennington		•	•						•		•	•		•	•
Middlebury College, Middlebury								•	•				•	•	•

	Accreditation	Architecture	Art Teaching	Fabric Design	Graphic Design	Illustration	Industrial Design	Interior Design	Painting	Photography	Printmaking	Sculpture	Men	Women	Scholarships
VIRGINIA															
Coll. of William & Mary, Williamsburg		•	•						•	•	•	•	•	•	•
Hollins College, Hollins College									•					•	
Richmond Professional Inst., Richmond			•	•	•	•	•	•	•	•	•	•	•	•	•
Univ. of Virginia, Charlottesville	N	•											•	•	
Virginia Polytechnic Inst., Blacksburg	N	•							•	•		•	•	•	•
WASHINGTON															
Central Wash. St. Coll., Ellensburg			•		•	•			•	•	•	•	•	•	
Eastern Wash. St. Coll., Cheney			•		•			•	•		•	•	•	•	
Univ. of Wash., Seattle	AN	•	•		•	•	•	•	•		•	•	•	•	•
Washington State Univ., Pullman		•	•		•	•		•	•		•	•	•	•	•
Western Wash. St. Coll., Bellingham			•						•		•	•	•	•	•
Whitworth College, Spokane			•						•	•	•	•	•	•	
WISCONSIN															
Layton School of Art, Milwaukee	A				•	•	•	•	•	•		•	•	•	•
Laurence University, Appleton		•							•				•	•	•
Mt. Mary College, Milwaukee			•	•				•	•		•			•	•
University of Wisconsin, Madison			•	•	•	•		•	•	•	•	•	•	•	•
Wisconsin State Univ., Superior			•		•				•	•	•	•	•	•	•

20
Professional Organizations and Guidance Agencies

At the beginning of this book, I listed the professional organizations, government agencies, and other groups who were helpful in compiling and editing *Art Career Guide*. They may also be helpful to you. Here are the names and addresses of professional organizations that may be able to supply further information about their particular fields.

American Association
of University Professors
1785 Massachusetts Avenue, NW
Washington 6, D. C.

American Institute of Architects
1735 New York Avenue, NW
Washington 6, D. C.

American Institute
of Graphic Arts
1059 Third Avenue
New York, New York 10021

American Institute
of Interior Designers
673 Fifth Avenue
New York, New York 10022

American Society
of Magazine Photographers
1472 Broadway
New York, New York 10036

Artists Equity Association
229 Broadway North
Seattle 2, Washington

Industrial Designers Society
of America
60 West 55th Street
New York, New York 10019

National Architectural
Accrediting Board
1620 Chemical Building
St. Louis 1, Missouri

National Art Education
Association
1201 16th Street, NW
Washington 6, D. C.

National Education Association
1201 16th Street, NW
Washington 6, D. C.

National Society of Art Directors
115 East 40th Street
New York, New York 10016

National Society
of Interior Designers
157 West 57th Street
New York, New York 10019

Professional Photographers
of America
152 West Wisconsin Avenue
Milwaukee 3, Wisconsin

Society of Illustrators
128 East 63rd Street
New York, New York 10021

Lists of accredited guidance agencies throughout the United States may be obtained from:

American Personnel and
Guidance Association
1605 New Hampshire Ave., NW
Washington 9, D. C.

American Psychological
Association
1333 16th Street, NW
Washington 6, D. C.

Two government agencies publish very useful material. The Labor Department issues excellent fact sheets on careers in the Occupational Outlook series. The Office of Education has material on schools and the teaching profession:

Bureau of Labor Statistics
United States Department
of Labor
Washington 25, D. C.

Office of Education
United States Department
of Health, Education and Welfare
Washington 25, D. C.